Hezekiah Butterworth

The Story of the Hymns - Or Hymns that Have a History

An Account of the Origin of Hymns of Personal Religious Experience

Hezekiah Butterworth

The Story of the Hymns - Or Hymns that Have a History
An Account of the Origin of Hymns of Personal Religious Experience

ISBN/EAN: 9783744780940

Printed in Europe, USA, Canada, Australia, Japan

Cover: Foto ©Thomas Meinert / pixelio.de

More available books at **www.hansebooks.com**

THE

Story of the Hymns;

OR

HYMNS THAT HAVE A HISTORY.

AN ACCOUNT OF THE ORIGIN OF HYMNS OF PERSONAL RELIGIOUS EXPERIENCE.

BY HEZEKIAH BUTTERWORTH.

AMERICAN TRACT SOCIETY,

150 NASSAU STREET, NEW YORK.

CONTENTS

II. HISTORICAL AND PERSONAL.

III. SONGS IN THE PILGRIMAGE.

IV. ORIGIN OF FAVORITE SUNDAY-SCHOOL HYMNS.

V. SEAMEN'S HYMNS.

VI. INDIAN HYMNS.

VII. RECENT HYMN-WRITERS AND THEIR HYMNS.

———+———

VIII. *AUTO-BIOGRAPHICAL HYMNS.*

———+———

IX. *FAMILIAR HYMNS, AUTHORS, DATES, ETC.* 245

———+———

X. *HYMN WRITERS, AND THEIR HYMNS* 267

PREFACE.

In preparing the "Story of the Hymns" the writer does not aim, like Miller, in his "Singers and Songs of the Church," to give a complete or nearly complete history of the origin of all hymns in common use, but only of such as are the result of some peculiar circumstance or special religious experience. The hymns that the church best loves, and most carefully preserves, are, for the most part, the fruit of eventful lives, luminous religious experiences, severe discipline, or unusual sorrow. It is the writer's object to associate such hymns with the peculiar circumstances that inspired them, and to explain the personal and local allusions that enter largely into their composition. The volume might properly have been called "The Origin of Hymns of Religious Experience."

Confidence adds largely to the enjoyment of what we read, and nothing more tends to increase our confidence in any literary composition than to know that the author wrote as he felt, and teaches what he himself has experienced. Nearly all works, written merely for effect, are ephemeral. The tinsel of fancy and mere sentiment fades, while words coined from the heart's pure gold live with the ages.

The sacred writers were careful to preserve the history of

nearly every psalm, from that of Miriam, when Pharaoh and his host were destroyed, to those of Mary in the presence of Elizabeth and Simeon in the Temple. We better understand the awful and shadowy grandeur of the ninetieth psalm, when it is explained to us that it is the "prayer which Moses the man of God prayed" after the people had sinned in the wilderness. We can enter into the spirit of the eighth psalm, which describes the sublimity of the celestial scenery at night, with a clearer insight when we are told that it was written by the shepherd of Bethlehem, after he had proved himself victorious over the melancholy of Saul at home, and over the champion of the Philistines in the field. It interests us to know that the first psalm was written for the jubilant assembly of King Asa, that the forty-fifth connects itself with the splendors of the reign of Jehoshaphat, that the twenty-fourth and twenty-fifth celebrate the removal of the ark after the conquest of Jerusalem, and that the thirtieth was written for the dedication of the House of David. So also in regard to the psalms that belong to the reign of Hezekiah, and refer to the destruction of the Assyrians; and the great Hebrew choral, or one hundred and seventh psalm, sung at the Feast of the Tabernacles.

Poets are the song-birds of human nature, the interpreters of human feeling; and they only are worthy of the name, in whose interpretations we find our own unexpressed thoughts and feelings and experiences. The sacred poet, like the Levite of old, is still a minister in the temple; he still kindles the altar fires of holy feeling, and from his own spiritual indwelling, insight, and inner communings, he puts into language for us those emotions, dispositions, desires, that our hearts recognize and yet our lips fail of uttering. He takes us to mountain tops of feeling, into valleys of shadow, and leads by streams of refreshing, and into solitudes of restfulness and calm. But to understand him best, we must know the ways by which he himself has been led, and have the assurance that it is a trusty guide with whom we enter into holy companionship.

The essential marks of a good hymn, remarks Earl Nelson, are, "1. It must be full of Scripture. 2. Full of individual life and reality. 3. It must have the acceptance of the use of the church. 4. It must be pure in its English, in its rhyme and its rhythm." He adds: "A hymn coming from a deep communing with God, and from the special experience of the human heart, at once fulfils, and only can fulfil, the tests I have ventured to lay down."

The number of hymns in the language is very large. Sir Roundell Palmer estimates that the hymns of Watts, Browne, Doddridge, Charles Wesley, Newton, Beddome, Kelly, and Montgomery, number 6,500; and Mr. Sedgwick, an English writer on hymns, published in 1861 a catalogue of 618 authors who are represented in various English hymn-books.

Of these hymns, only the fittest survive, and the most helpful stand the test of time. It usually happens that the most painstaking and elaborate productions of the Christian lyrist are the first to perish, while some minor expression of sincere religious feeling is the surest to live, and take its place among the recognized lyrics of the church.

The larger portion of the hymns whose history is given in this volume is familiar to all who have had the training of the Christian church. The religious experiences out of which these hymns grew are not as familiar to those who have not made a special study of the subject. That the book may lead some to better know the guides of their spiritual journey, whose experiences almost daily mingle with their own in the sweet sympathies of song, is the devout wish of the author.

I. TONES IN THE CHURCH.

1. *ALL HAIL THE POWER OF JESUS' NAME.*
2. *A MIGHTY FORTRESS IS OUR GOD.*
3. *PRAISE GOD FROM WHOM ALL BLESSINGS FLOW.*
4. *KEN'S MORNING HYMN.*
5. *KEN'S EVENING HYMN.*
6. *ROCK OF AGES, CLEFT FOR ME!*
7. *FULL ASSURANCE.*
8. *GUIDE ME, O THOU GREAT JEHOVAH.*
9. *LORD OF THE SABBATH, HEAR OUR VOWS.*
10. *COME, YE SINNERS, POOR AND NEEDY.*
11. *BLEST BE THE TIE THAT BINDS.*
12. *FROM GREENLAND'S ICY MOUNTAINS.*
13. *MIGHTY GOD, WHILE ANGELS BLESS THEE.*
14. *FAR FROM THE WORLD.*
15. *GOD MOVES IN A MYSTERIOUS WAY.*
16. *I LOVE TO STEAL A WHILE AWAY.*
17. *WHEN ALL THY MERCIES, O MY GOD.*
18. *O THOU, MY SOUL, FORGET NO MORE.*
19. *JESUS, MY ALL, TO HEAVEN IS GONE.*
20. *FATHER, WHATE'ER OF EARTHLY BLISS.*
21. *JESUS, AND SHALL IT EVER BE!*
22. *VITAL SPARK OF HEAVENLY FLAME.*

TONES IN THE CHURCH.

"ALL HAIL THE POWER OF JESUS' NAME."

EDWARD PERRONET, the author of the most inspiring and triumphant hymn in the English language, is a benefactor whose history is but little known. He was a man of great humility of character, but was sustained amid many vicissitudes of life by an all-victorious faith.

He was the son of Rev. Vincent Perronet, an excellent English clergyman of the old school, who was vicar of Shoreham for fifty years. He left the established church in early life, and became a Methodist. He was a bosom friend of Rev. Charles Wesley, in whose diary mention of him may be found, beginning about the year 1750. He was one of the preachers appointed under the patronage of the Countess of Huntingdon, and, adding an ardent zeal to a humble and sympathetic nature, his labors in the ministry were for a time attended with marked success. But Perronet was at heart an opponent of the union of church and state, and at last produced an anonymous poem entitled the " Mitre," a keen satire on the national establishment. This hostility brought him under the displeasure of the countess. He severed his connection with her society, and became the pastor of a small congregation of Dissenters, to whom he preached till his death, which took place in January, 1792.

His death was triumphant, and is an evidence of the sincerity of the piety which inspired his rapturous hymn. His majestic faith seemed to lift his soul above the world, and to antedate that coronation day when the cherubic hosts and the redeemed shall

> "Bring forth the royal diadem,
> And crown Him Lord of all!"

His dying testimony was:

> "Glory to God in the height of his divinity!
> Glory to God in the depth of his humanity!
> Glory to God in his all-sufficiency!
> Unto his hands I commend my spirit."

The following is the original version of Perronet's jubilant hymn, which has become one of the grandest as well as the most familiar tones of the church:

> ALL hail the power of Jesus' name!
> Let angels prostrate fall;
> Bring forth the royal diadem,
> To crown him Lord of all.
>
> Crown him, ye martyrs of your God,
> Who from his altar call;
> Extol the Stem of Jesse's rod,
> And crown him Lord of all.
>
> Hail him, ye heirs of David's line,
> Whom David "Lord" did call;
> The God incarnate! Man divine!
> And crown him Lord of all!

Ye seed of Israel's chosen race,
  Ye ransomed of the fall,
Hail him who saves you by his grace,
  And crown him Lord of all.

Sinners, whose love can ne'er forget
  The wormwood and the gall,
Go, spread your trophies at his feet,
  And crown him Lord of all.

Let every tribe and every tongue
  That bound creation's call,
Now shout the universal song,
  The crownéd Lord of all.

"*A MIGHTY FORTRESS IS OUR GOD.*"

S. T. COLERIDGE says that Martin Luther did as much for the Reformation by his hymns, as by his translation of the Bible. The hymns of Luther were indeed the battle-cry and trumpet-call of the Reformation: "The children learned them in the cottage, and martyrs sung them on the scaffold."

The hymn beginning

"Ein' feste Burg ist unser Gott,"

is the grandest of Luther's hymns, and is in harmony with sublime historical periods, from its very nature, boldness, and sublimity. It was written, according to Welles, in the memorable year when the evangelical princes delivered their protest at the Diet of Spires, from which the word and the meaning of the word "Protestant" is derived. "Luther used often to sing it in 1530, while the Diet of Augsburg was sitting. It soon became the favorite psalm with the people. It was one of the watchwords of the Reformation, cheering armies to conflict, and sustaining believers in the hours of fiery trial.

"After Luther's death, when his affectionate coadjutor Melancthon was at Weimar with his banished friends Jonas and Creuziger, he heard a little maid singing this psalm in the street, and said, 'Sing on, my little girl, you little know whom you comfort.' The first line of this hymn is inscribed on Luther's tomb at Wittenburg."

> A MIGHTY fortress is our God,
>   A bulwark never failing;
> Our helper he, amid the flood
>   Of mortal ills prevailing.
> For still our ancient foe
> Doth seek to work us woe;
> His craft and power are great,
> And, armed with cruel hate,
>   On earth is not his equal.
>
> Did we in our own strength confide,
>   Our striving would be losing—
> Were not the right man on our side,
>   The man of God's own choosing.
> Dost ask, who that may be?
> Christ Jesus, it is he;
> His name Lord Sabaoth,
> Our God and Saviour both,
>   He shall our souls deliver.
>
> And though this world, with devils filled,
>   Should threaten to undo us,
> We will not fear, for God hath willed
>   His truth to triumph through us.

The Prince of Darkness grim—
We tremble not for him :
His rage we can endure,
For lo! his doom is sure,
  One little word shall fell him.

That word above all earthly powers—
  No thanks to them—abideth ;
The Spirit and the gifts are ours,
  Through Him who with us sideth.
Let goods and kindred go,
This mortal life also ;
The body they may kill,
God's truth abideth still,
  His kingdom is for ever.

"PRAISE GOD FROM WHOM ALL BLESSINGS FLOW."

THE grand doxology, beginning,

  "Praise God, from whom all blessings flow,"

is suited to all religious occasions, to all Christian denominations, to all times, places, and conditions of men,
and has been translated into all civilized tongues, and
adopted by the church universal. Written more than
two hundred years ago, it has become the grandest tone
in the anthem of earth's voices continually rising to
heaven. As England's drum-call follows the sun, so the
tongues that take up this grateful ascription of praise
are never silent, but incessantly encircle the earth with
their melody.

Thomas Ken, (Kenn,) the writer of the hymns that
first contained this magnificent stanza, in the form that

it is now used, was born at Berkhamstead, England, in 1637, and was educated at Oxford.   He early in life consecrated himself to God, and became a prelate.   He was a lover of holy music.   The organists and choristers being silenced by the rigid rule of Cromwell, musical societies were formed, in one of which Ken played the lute with admirable skill.   This society was accustomed to meet in the college chambers.

The Morning and the Evening Hymn, which end with this doxology, were originally written for the use of the students in Winchester College, and were appended to a devotional work which he himself prepared, entitled "The Manual of Prayers."   In this latter work he thus counsels the young men of the college : "Be sure to sing the Morning and Evening Hymns in your chamber, devoutly remembering that the Psalmist upon happy experience assures you that it is a good thing to tell of the loving kindness of the Lord early in the morning and of his truth in the night season."   These hymns were probably at first printed on broad sheets of paper and sent to each student's room.   They were added to the Manual for Prayer in 1697.   The work was now entitled, " A Manual of Prayers for the Use of Scholars in Winchester College and all other devout Christians ; to which are added Three Hymns, Morning, Evening, and Midnight, not in former editions, by the same author."

In 1679, Ken was appointed chaplain to Mary, Princess of Orange, and in 1680 chaplain to Charles II. In the latter capacity he fearlessly did his duty, as one accountable to God alone, and not to any man.   He reproved the "merry monarch" for his vices, in the plainest and most direct manner. "I must go and hear Ken tell me my faults," the king used to say good-humoredly. In 1684, Charles raised him to the see of Bath and Wells.

"Before he became a bishop," says Macaulay, "he had maintained the honor of his gown by refusing, when the court was at Winchester, to let Nell Gwynn, the king's mistress, lodge at the house which he occupied as prebendary. The king had sense enough to respect so manly a spirit. Of all the prelates he liked Ken best." Charles once spoke of him as the "good little man that refused his lodgings to poor little Nell."

He was the faithful spiritual adviser of Charles II. on his death-bed, and attended the Duke of Monmouth at his execution. He resisted the reëstablishment of popery under James, and was one of the famous "seven bishops" who were tried for treason and acquitted. Having sworn allegiance to James, he was too conscientious to break his oath on the ascension of William III., Prince of Orange, and was deprived of his bishopric as a non-juror at the coronation.

He was now reduced to poverty, a condition not unacceptable to him, for he was not allured by the false glitter of the courts of kings. Like Fenelon, in retiring from places of splendor and power, he loved to be alone with his God, and let the world play its drama without being an actor. He was invited by Lord Viscount Weymouth to spend the remainder of his days in his mansion at Longleat, near Frome, in Somersetshire. There, enjoying the hospitality of a small suite of rooms, he lived in happy retirement for twenty years, universally respected and beloved. Queen Anne offered to restore him to the see of Bath and Wells, but he declined the position, "with grateful thanks for her majesty's gracious remembrance of him, having long since determined to remain in privacy."

He died in March, 1710, and was buried in the churchyard of Frome. He had requested that six of the poorest men of the parish might carry him to his grave, and that he might be interred without pomp or ceremony. This accordingly was the manner of his burial.

"The moral character of Ken," says Lord Macaulay, "when impartially reviewed, sustains a comparison with any in ecclesiastical history, and seems to approach, as near as any human infirmity permits, to the ideal of Christian perfection."

KEN'S MORNING HYMN.

ORIGINAL TEXT OF 1697.

AWAKE, my soul, and with the sun
Thy daily stage of duty run;
Shake off dull sloth, and early rise
To pay thy morning sacrifice.

Redeem thy misspent time that 's past,
And live this day as if thy last;
Improve thy talent with due care,
'Gainst the great day thyself prepare.

Let all thy converse be sincere,
Thy conscience as the noonday clear;
Think how all-seeing GOD thy ways
And all thy secret thoughts surveys.

Influenced of the Light divine
Let thine own light in good works shine;
Reflect all heaven's propitious rays
In ardent love and cheerful praise.

Wake and lift up thyself, my heart,
And with the angels bear thy part,
Who all night long unwearied sing
Glory to the Eternal King.

I wake, I wake, ye heavenly choir,
May your devotion me inspire,
That I like you my age may spend,
Like you may on my GOD attend.

May I like you in GOD delight,
Have all day long my GOD in sight,
Perform like you my Maker's will,
Oh may I never more do ill.

Had I your wings to heaven I 'd fly;
But GOD shall that defect supply,
And my soul, winged with warm desire,
Shall all day long to heaven aspire.

Glory to thee who safe hast kept,
And hast refreshed me while I slept;
Grant, Lord, when I from death shall wake,
I may of endless light partake.

I would not wake, nor rise again,
E'en heaven itself I would disdain,
Wert not thou there to be enjoyed,
And I in hymns to be employed.

Heaven is, dear Lord, where'er thou art;
Oh never then from me depart;
For to my soul 't is hell to be,
But for a moment without thee.

Lord, I my vows to thee renew ;
Scatter my sins as morning dew;
Guard my first springs of thought and will,
And with thyself my spirit fill.

Direct, control, suggest this day,
All I design, or do, or say ;
That all my powers, with all their might
In thy sole glory may unite.

Praise God, from whom all blessings flow :
Praise Him, all creatures here below;
Praise Him above, ye angelic host,
Praise Father, Son and Holy Ghost.

———◆———

KEN'S EVENING HYMN.

ORIGINAL TEXT OF 1697.

GLORY to Thee, my GOD, this night
For all the blessings of the light;
Keep me, oh keep me, KING of kings,
Under thine own Almighty wings.

Forgive me, LORD, for thy dear SON,
The ills that I this day have done,
That with the world, myself, and thee,
I, ere I sleep, at peace may be.

Teach me to live, that I may dread
The grave as little as my bed ;
Teach me to die, that so I may
Triumphing rise at the last day.

Oh may my soul on thee repose,
And may sweet sleep mine eyelids close,
Sleep that shall me more vigorous make
To serve my GOD when I awake.

When in the night I sleepless lie,
My soul with heavenly thoughts supply;
Let no ill dreams disturb my rest,
No powers of darkness me molest.

Dull sleep, of sense me to deprive!
I am but half my days alive;
Thy faithful lovers, Lord, are grieved
To lie so long of thee bereaved.

But though sleep o'er my frailty reigns,
Let it not hold me long in chains,
And now and then let loose my heart,
Till it a hallelujah dart.

The faster sleep the sense does bind,
The more unfettered is the mind,
Oh may my soul, from matter free,
Thy unveiled goodness waking see.

Oh when shall I, in endless day,
For ever chase dark sleep away,
And endless praise with the heavenly choir
Incessant sing, and never tire?

You, my blest guardian, whilst I sleep,
Close to my bed your vigils keep,
Divine love into me instil,
Stop all the avenues of ill.

Thought to thought with my soul converse,
Celestial joys to me rehearse,
And in my stead all the night long,
Sing to my God a grateful song.

Praise GOD from whom all blessings flow:
Praise Him all creatures here below:
Praise Him above, ye angelic host:
Praise FATHER, SON, and HOLY GHOST.

"ROCK OF AGES."

THE hymn beginning,

> "Rock of Ages, cleft for me,"

may well be esteemed one of the brightest gems of Christian psalmody. It holds a place in the affections of the church, second, perhaps, only to Charles Wesley's deep spiritual petition,

> "Jesus, lover of my soul."

It is a grand tone that nerves and strengthens faith, that associates the sublime imagery of the Hebrew Scriptures with the all-protecting love of Christ, and that has consoled thousands of Christians in the dying hour. The late Prince Consort repeated the first stanza on his bed of death, and found in it the perfect interpretation of the sentiment of his hopeful Christian experience.

Augustus Montague Toplady, the author, was born at Farnham, Surrey, England in 1740. His father fell at the battle of Carthagena, and he was brought up in charge of an exemplary and pious mother. He was educated at Westminster school.

At the age of sixteen, Toplady chanced to go into a barn at an obscure place, called Codymain, Ireland, to hear an illiterate layman preach. The sermon made upon him an unexpected impression and led to his immediate conversion. He thus speaks of this interesting experience in his diary: "That sweet text, 'Ye who sometime were afar off are made nigh by the blood of Christ.' was particularly delightful and refreshing to my soul. It was from that passage that Mr. Morris preached on the memorable evening of my effectual call by the grace of God, under the ministry of that dear messenger, under that sermon, I was, I trust, brought nigh by the blood of Christ, in August, 1756.

" Strange that I, who had so long been under the means of grace in England, should be brought nigh to God in an obscure part of Ireland, amidst a handful of God's people met together in a barn, and under the ministry of one who could scarcely spell his name. The excellency of such power must be of God and cannot be of men."

He became a minister of the church of England, maintained the Calvinistic doctrines in opposition to the Wesleys, and preached and wrote with self-consuming zeal. The only blemish of his high character was heated language and intolerance in controversy.

In the year 1775 his health began to fail. It was evident that the sword was too sharp for the scabbard. His physical energies were being destroyed by the fiery ardor of soul that over-taxed them. His physician commanded him to go to London. Here a new field opened before him, and he became pastor of the French Calvinist Reformed Church.

On the year of his settlement in London, he published in the *Gospel Magazine* (March, 1776) an article, entitled " Questions and Answers Relative to the National Debt," in which he adverts to the debt of sin, and shows how multitudinous are the sins of mankind. By numerical calculations, he exhibits the enormity of the debt of the redeemed soul, which Christ has cancelled, and impresses

the reader with the transcendent love and value of Christ's
atonement.   With these thoughts glowing like a vision
in his mind, he then added :

> Rock of ages, cleft for me,
> Let me hide myself in thee;
> Let the water and the blood,
> From thy riven side which flowed,
> Be of sin the double cure,
> Cleanse me from its guilt and power.
>
> Not the labor of my hands
> Can fulfil thy law's demands;
> Could my zeal no respite know,
> Could my tears for ever flow,
> All for sin could not atone,
> Thou must save, and thou alone.
>
> Nothing in my hand I bring,
> Simply to thy cross I cling;
> Naked, come to thee for dress,
> Helpless, look to thee for grace;
> Foul, I to the fountain fly;
> Wash me, Saviour, or I die.
>
> Whilst I draw this fleeting breath,
> When my eyestrings break in death;
> When I soar through tracts unknown,
> See thee on thy judgment throne,
> Rock of ages, cleft for me,
> Let me hide myself in thee.

The above is the original version, from which it will
be seen that the hymn in common use has been greatly
transposed and altered.

It was composed in Toplady's last years, when he
already felt that he was beginning to lose his hold on

life, and that his feet were already standing on celestial altitudes. Some two years afterwards, when he was yet but thirty-eight years of age, the full time of his departure came, and he found the prayer in the last stanza of his hymn fully and sweetly answered in the revelation of Divine love to his soul. He seemed to walk in Beulah, to breathe immortal airs and to hear the tuning of unseen harps, and by faith to discover what the Protomartyr saw and the Revelator described.

"Your pulse," said the doctor, "is becoming weaker."

"That is a good sign," said Toplady, "that my death is fast approaching, and I can add that my heart beats every day stronger and stronger for glory."

As his end drew immediately near, tears of joy filled his eyes, before which already seemed to pass visions of Paradise, and he exclaimed: "It will not be long before God takes me, for no mortal can live after the glories God has manifested to my soul."

The following hymn, which furnishes a picture of his religious consolations, confidence and hope, was written during one of these periods of illness, that gradually wasted his strength, and brought him constantly in face with death and the eternal world:

> When languor and disease invade
>   This trembling house of clay,
> 'T is sweet to look beyond my pains,
>   And long to fly away;
>
> Sweet to look inward, and attend
>   The whispers of his love;
> Sweet to look upward, to the place
>   Where Jesus pleads above:

Sweet to look back, and see my name
  In life's fair book set down ;
Sweet to look forward, and behold
  Eternal joys my own ;

Sweet to reflect how grace divine
  My sins on Jesus laid ;
Sweet to remember that his blood
  My debt of suffering paid ;

Sweet to rejoice in lively hope,
  That, when my change shall come,
Angels shall hover round my bed,
  And waft my spirit home.

If such the sweetness of the stream,
  What must the fountain be,
Where saints and angels draw their bliss
  Directly, Lord, from thee.

———◆———

The following Latin version of Rock of Ages, is by
Rt. Hon. W. E. Gladstone :

Jesus, pro me perforatus,
Condar intra tuum latus ;
Tu per lympham profluentem,
Tu per sanguinem tepentem,
In peccata mî redunda,
Tolle culpam, sordes munda !

Coram Te nec justus forem
Quamvis totâ vi laborem,
Nec si fide nunquam cesso,
Fletu stillans indefesso ;
Tibi soli tantum munus—
Salva me, Salvator Unus !

Nil in manu mecum fero,
Sed me versus crucem gero:
Vestimenta nudus oro,
Opem debilis imploro,
Fontem CHRISTI quæro immundus,
Nisi laves, moribundus.

Dum hos artus vita regit,
Quando nox sepulcro tegit;
Mortuos quum stare jubes,
Sedens Judex inter nubes;—
JESUS, pro me perforatus,
Condar intra tuum latus!

———◆———

The following hymn, by Toplady, is not found in many of the standard hymn-books:

FULL ASSURANCE.

A DEBTOR to mercy alone,
  Of covenant mercy I sing,
Nor fear, with thy righteousness on,
  My person and offering to bring.

The terrors of law and of God
  With me can have nothing to do,
My Saviour's obedience and blood
  Hide all my transgressions from view.

The work which his goodness began,
  The arm of his strength will complete;
His promise is yea and amen,
  And never was forfeited yet.

Things future, nor things that are now,
  Nor all things below nor above,
Can make him his purpose forego, .
  Or sever my soul from his love.

3*

My name from the palms of his hands
Eternity cannot erase,
Impressed on his heart it remains,
In marks of indelible grace.

Yes, I to the end shall endure,
As sure as the earnest is given;
More happy, but not more secure,
The glorified spirits in heaven.

----+----

"GUIDE ME, O THOU GREAT JEHOVAH."

THE much-used hymn, beginning,

"Guide me, O thou great Jehovah!"

is attributed to Olivers in nearly all American collections of hymns. We find it so credited in some of the more careful compilations, among them, "Hymns for the Church Militant." It was written by William Williams, a Welsh preacher in the Welsh Calvinist-Methodist connection, in the times of Whitefield and Lady Huntingdon. Olivers, who was a musician as well as a poet, and himself a Welshman, supplied the music, and so his name became accidentally associated with the authorship of the hymn.

William Williams, or Williams of Pantycelyn, who has been called the Watts of Wales, was born in 1717, in the parish of Llanfair-ar-y-bryn, in Carmarthenshire.

His conversion forms an interesting part of his student-history. He was awakened to the importance of personal religion while listening to the words of the once famous preacher, Howel Harris, in Talgarth churchyard.

His experience was a clear one, and the duty of becoming a preacher was made plain to him. He received deacon's orders at the age of twenty-three. At the age of thirty-two he left the Established Church and became an itinerant Methodist preacher.

He possessed the warm heart and glowing imagination of a true Welshman, and his sermons abounded with vivid picturing, and, always radiant with the presence of his Divine Master, they produced an extraordinary effect on susceptible Welshmen.

Working in connection with such zealous ministers as Harris and Rowlands, he became a very popular preacher, and his local fame greatly increased when to Welsh eloquence he added the choicest gifts of song, and began to publish his highly experimental hymns. The inspiring words of

"O'er the gloomy hills of darkness,"

were written long before the beginning of foreign missionary enterprises, while Williams, its popular author, was yet traversing the lonely mountains of Wales, and looking for the dawn of a brighter religious day. Welshmen sung the hymn as a prophecy, and felt their hearts gladdened with hope, years and years before the church begun her aggressive march into pagan and heathen lands.

His first Welsh hymn-book was entitled the "Alleluia," and was printed in Bristol in six parts in 1745-'47. His second book was called "The Sea of Glass," and the third, "Visible Farewell; Welcome to Invisible Things."

In 1771 he wrote an elegy on Whitefield, which he dedicated to the Countess of Huntingdon. He died in 1791.

It is probable that the famous hymn, beginning, "Guide me, O thou great Jehovah," was sung in America before it obtained a European reputation. Its history is as follows: Lady Huntingdon having read one of Williams' books with much spiritual satisfaction, persuaded him to prepare a collection of hymns, to be called the "Gloria in Excelsis," for especial use in Mr. Whitefield's Orphans' House in America. In this collection appeared the original stanzas of "Guide me, O thou great Jehovah." In 1774, two years after its publication in the "Gloria in Excelsis," it was republished in England in Mr. Whitefield's collections of hymns. Its rendering from the Welsh into English is attributed to W. Evans, who gives a rendering similar to that found in the present collections of hymns. The hymn was taken up by the Calvinist-Methodists, embodying as it did a metrical prayer for God's overcoming strength and victorious deliverance in life's hours of discipline and trial, expressed in truly majestic language, in harmony with a firm religious reliance and trust, and a lofty experimental faith. It immediately became popular among all denominations of Christians, holding a place in the affections of the church with Robinson's "Come, thou Fount of every blessing." (It is now usually sung to "Greenville," the music of which is nearly identical with Rousseau's "Dream," and which was composed by Rousseau. Its original music, as we have said, was written by Thomas Olivers.

The original hymn had four stanzas, and was some-what stronger in the choice of words than the present popular verses.   It was as follows:

> Guide me, O thou great Jehovah,
>   Pilgrim through this barren land:
> I am weak, but thou art mighty,
>   Hold me by thy powerful hand;
>   Bread of heaven,
> Feed me till I want no more.
>
> Open now the crystal fountain,
>   Whence the healing streams do flow;
> Let the fiery, cloudy pillar
>   Guide me all my journey through;
>   Strong Deliverer,
> Be thou still my strength and shield.
>
> When I tread the verge of Jordan,
>   Bid my anxious fears subside;
> Death of death, and hell's destruction,
>   Land me safe on Canaan's side.
>   Songs of praises
> I will ever give to thee.
>
> Musing on my habitation,
>   Musing on my heavenly home,
> Fills my heart with holy longing;
>   Come, Lord Jesus, quickly come.
>   Vanity is all I see,
> Lord, I long to be with thee.

Most versions read in the second line of the second stanza, "Whence the crystal waters flow," which presents to the mind a picture inferior to the original.   In the third stanza the third line usually reads, "Bear me through the swelling current," which is also an inferior picture for the singer, whatever it may be to the rhetorician. The last stanza is fervent, confident, and strong, lifting the soul on the wings of aspiration and faith, and it seems rather remarkable that it should be so commonly omitted.

"LORD OF THE SABBATH, HEAR OUR VOWS."

WHEN Dr. Doddridge, during his useful ministry, had finished the preparation of a pulpit discourse that strongly impressed him, he was accustomed, while his heart was yet glowing with the sentiment that had inspired him, to put the principal thoughts into metre, and use the hymn thus written at the conclusion of the preaching of the sermon. At the close of a discourse preached in Jan. 2, 1736, from the text, " There remaineth therefore a rest to the people of God," he read the beautiful hymn, containing the following almost unequalled stanzas :

> Thine earthly Sabbaths, Lord, we love,
> But there's a nobler rest above;
> To that our laboring souls aspire,
> With ardent hope and strong desire.
>
> No more fatigue, no more distress,
> Nor sin nor hell shall reach the place;
> No sighs shall mingle with the songs
> Which warble from immortal tongues.
>
> No rude alarms of raging foes;
> No cares to break the long repose;
> No midnight shade, no clouded sun,
> But sacred, high, eternal noon.

> O long-expected day, begin;
> Dawn on these realms of woe and sin:
> Fain would we leave this weary road,
> And sleep in death, to rest with God.

Dr. Doddridge, in his last years, seemed to have a spiritual foretaste of the heavenly joy and rest. Embarking for Lisbon, in the hope of benefit from warmer air, he was able to say to his wife in his cabin, when conscious that his life was almost ended, these cheerful and triumphant words: "I cannot express to you what a morning I have had. Such delightful and transporting views of the heavenly world as my Father is now indulging me with, no words can express." He died at Lisbon of consumption, in his fiftieth year. He anticipated to the last the glorious rest he sings in his hymn.

------◆------

"*COME, YE SINNERS, POOR AND NEEDY.*"

FEW hymns for the last hundred years have been more frequently sung, at times of special spiritual refreshing, than that beginning,

> "Come, ye sinners, poor and needy."

It was written under the inspiration of a somewhat remarkable religious experience. Joseph Hart, its author, was born in London in 1712. He was liberally educated, and commenced life as a teacher. At times, in early manhood, he was deeply interested in the subject of religion, and led a restrained and prayerful life. But he fell a victim to temptation, engaged in many evil practices, and gained an unenviable notoriety for his disregard of decency and religious truth. "I was," he said, "in an abominable state, a loose backslider, and an audacious apostate." He published heathen translations of a pernicious tendency, and a skeptical work, entitled, "The Unreasonableness of Religion."

His conscious errors and lapses were followed by terrible compunctions of conscience, and these inward tortures, which gave him no peace, led at last to his reformation. He now began in earnest to seek the Saviour. After a period of great mental distress, he met with a change of heart, and experienced an abiding sense of the pardoning love of God. This happy change was wrought by his receiving a profound impression of the sufferings of Christ. He says, "The week before Easter, 1757, I had such an amazing view of the agony of Christ in the garden as I know not how well to describe. I was lost in wonder and adoration, and the impression was too deep, I believe, ever to be obliterated. I believe that no one can know anything of the sufferings of Jesus, but by the Holy Ghost." Under the influence of this experience he composed the first part of the hymn beginning,

"Come, all ye chosen saints of God."

This experience he has very vividly impressed upon his well-known hymn, "Come, ye sinners, poor and needy."

ORIGINAL.

Come, ye sinners, poor and wretched,
  Weak and wounded, sick and sore;
Jesus ready stands to save you,
  Full of pity joined with power;
      He is able,
  He is willing; doubt no more.

Come, ye needy, come and welcome,
  God's free bounty glorify :
True belief and true repentance,
  Every grace that brings you nigh,
    Without money,
  Come to Jesus Christ and buy.

Come, ye weary, heavy-laden,
  Bruised and broken by the fall,
If you tarry till you 're better,
  You will never come at all :
    Not the righteous,
  Sinners Jesus came to call.

View him grov'ling in the garden ;
  Lo, your Maker prostrate lies ;
On the bloody tree behold him !
  Hear him cry, before he dies,
    " It is finished !"
  Sinners, will not this suffice ?

Lo ! the incarnate God, ascended,
  Pleads the merit of his blood ;
Venture on him—venture wholly,
  Let no other trust intrude ;
    None but Jesus
  Can do helpless sinners good.

"*BLEST BE THE TIE THAT BINDS.*"

PERHAPS the best poetical expression of the sentiment of Christian brotherhood in the English language
is found in the hymn beginning,

  " Blest be the tie that binds
    Our hearts in Christian love."

John Fawcett, D. D., the author of this hymn, a
name that finds frequent place in Baptist collections of

church psalmody, was born near Bradford, Yorkshire, January 6, 1739. At the age of sixteen, while an apprentice, he heard Mr. Whitefield preach. The sermon was instrumental in his conversion, and he joined the Methodist Society. In 1758 he became a member of the newly-formed Baptist church in Bradford. Here his activity and usefulness were so great, that his brethren advised him " to go beyond private exhortation," and "to stand forth and preach the gospel." After much praying and many inward conflicts, he decided to follow their advice. In the summer of 1765, he was ordained minister of the Baptist Society at Wainsgate. His work here was hard ; but his zeal and far-reaching sympathies won the hearts of his people, and opened the way of pastoral success. In 1772, after a pastorate of seven years, in which he had steadily grown in the attachment of a prosperous society, he went to London to preach for Dr. Gill, who was about resigning his ministerial office on account of his age and infirmities. Dr. Gill's people were so much pleased with his deportment and discourses, that they gave him a call to become their pastor.

His church in Wainsgate was scattered and poor ; that in London was large, with ample resources, and presented a most promising field for a man with growing capacities. His goods were loaded for removal to London, and his parishioners assembled to bid him a final adieu. An affecting scene followed, the poor people he had so long instructed and befriended entreating him with tears to remain. The voice of love prevailed ; he was convinced that it was his duty to remain here, and that this was the field Providence had allotted him.

"I will stay," he said. "You may unpack my goods, and we will live for the Lord lovingly together."

The affectionate expression of regard on the part of his parishioners made a deep impression upon his mind, and inspired him to pen in return, under an impulse of true poetic feeling, his well-known hymn:

> Blest be the tie that binds
>   Our hearts in Christian love:
> The fellowship of kindred minds
>   Is like to that above.
>
> Before our Father's throne
>   We pour our ardent prayers:
> Our fears, our hopes, our aims are one—
>   Our comforts and our cares.
>
> We share our mutual woes;
>   Our mutual burdens bear
> And often for each other flows
>   The sympathizing tear.
>
> When we asunder part,
>   It gives us inward pain;
> But we shall still be joined in heart,
>   And hope to meet again.
>
> This glorious hope revives
>   Our courage by the way:
> While each in expectation lives,
>   And longs to see the day.
>
> From sorrow, toil, and pain,
>   And sin we shall be free;
> And perfect love and friendship reign
>   Through all eternity.

Dr. Fawcett was a great sufferer towards the close of his life ; but he seemed to dwell, as it were, on the confines of a better world, with the celestial country full in view. His last words were, "Come, Lord Jesus ; come quickly."

———◆———

"FROM GREENLAND'S ICY MOUNTAINS."

THE origin of this hymn is given in Bishop Heber's memoirs, and retold in the annotations to the Hymnal. We find in an American religious magazine a somewhat elegant version of the incident, which is as follows :

"It does not necessarily take a lifetime to accomplish immortality. A brave act done in a moment, a courageous word spoken at the fitting time, a few lines which can be written on a sheet of note-paper, may give one a deathless name. Such was the case with Reginald Heber, known far and wide, wherever the Christian religion has penetrated, by his unequalled missionary hymn, 'From Greenland's icy mountains.' These lines, so dear to every heart, so certain to live, while a benighted man remains to whom Christ's story has not yet been wafted, were written in a parlor, with conversation going on around its author, and in a few minutes' time.

"Reginald Heber, then thirty-five years old, was visiting his father-in-law, Dr. Shipley, in Wrexham, having left his own charge at Hodnet a short time in order to deliver some lectures in Dr. Shipley's church. Half a dozen friends were gathered in the little rectory parlor one Saturday afternoon, when Dr. Shipley turned to Heber, knowing the ease with which he composed, and

asked him if he could not write some missionary lines for his church to sing the next morning, as he was going to preach upon the subject of Missions. This was not very long notice to give to a man to achieve the distinguishing work of his life, and in the few moments which followed, Heber builded better than he knew. Retiring to a corner of the room, he wrote three verses of his hymn, and returning read them to his companions, only altering the one word, savage, to heathen in the second verse.

"'There, there,' said Dr. Shipley, 'that will do very well.' But Heber, replying that the sense was not quite complete, retired for a few moments, and then returned with the glorious bugle-blast of the fourth verse:

> "'Waft, waft, ye winds, His story,
> And you, ye waters, roll,
> Till like a sea of glory
> It spreads from pole to pole;
> Till o'er our ransomed nature
> The LAMB, for sinners slain,
> Redeemer, King, Creator,
> In bliss returns to reign. Amen.'

"It was printed that evening, and sung the next morning by the people of Wrexham church."

> From Greenland's icy mountains,
> From India's coral strand,
> Where Afric's sunny fountains
> Roll down their golden sand,
> From many an ancient river,
> From many a palmy plain,
> They call us to deliver
> Their land from error's chain.

What though the spicy breezes
　　Blow soft o'er Java's isle,
Though every prospect pleases,
　　And only man is vile ;
In vain, with lavish kindness,
　　The gifts of God are strewn ;
The heathen, in his blindness,
　　Bows down to wood and stone.

Can we, whose souls are lighted
　　By wisdom from on high,
Can we to man benighted
　　The lamp of life deny ?
Salvation ! O salvation !
　　The joyful sound proclaim,
Till earth's remotest nation
　　Has learned Messiah's name.

Waft, waft, ye winds, His story,
　　And you, ye waters, roll,
Till, like a sea of glory,
　　It spreads from pole to pole ;
Till o'er our ransomed nature
　　The Lamb, for sinners slain,
Redeemer, King, Creator,
　　In bliss returns to reign.

----•----

"MIGHTY GOD, WHILE ANGELS BLESS THEE."

ROBERT ROBINSON, the author of the well-known
hymn beginning,

"Come, thou Fount of every blessing,"

was a man of genius and impressible feelings, but was
easily influenced by the force of association or circumstance, an instability which he deeply regretted in his

declining years.   He was by turns a Methodist, an Independent, a Baptist, and a Socinian.   He once said to a lady whom he chanced to hear singing

"Come, thou Fount of every blessing,"

in a stage-coach, after his relapse into the gloomy speculations of Socinianism, "Madam, I am the poor, unhappy man who composed that hymn, many years ago; and I would give a thousand worlds, if I had them, to enjoy the feelings I had then."

The early Methodists produced a number of hymns, which, like the German lyrics written during the thirty years' war, illustrate the majesty of faith.   Among these are John Wesley's itinerant productions, Charles Wesley's famous hymn written on the Land's End, Cornwall, and Oliver's "The God of Abraham praise."

The well-known hymn beginning,

"Mighty God, while angels bless thee,"

belongs to the same class.   It was written under peculiar circumstances, and such as would seem to be little likely to inspire so noble a theme.

"It was composed," says Dr. Belcher, "for the use of Benjamin Williams, deacon of the Baptist church at Reading.   Benjamin was a favorite of Robinson when a boy.   One day the poet took the boy into his lap, and under the influence of that affectionate feeling which a child's love inspires, he wrote:

> "Mighty God, while angels bless thee,
>   May an infant praise thy name?
> Lord of men as well as angels,
>   Thou art every creature's theme."

So far the poet's mind seems to have been influenced by the child he was holding. But a warm glow of religious feeling was awakened within him, and the second stanza was one of remarkable fervor and power:

> "Lord of every land and nation,
> Ancient of eternal days,
> Sounded through the whole creation
> Be thy just and lawful praise.
> Hallelujah! Amen."

After completing the whole hymn, he read it to the child, and put it playfully into his hand. "Well do we remember," says Dr. Belcher, "the deep feeling with which Deacon Williams described to us the scene, as we sat with him by his own fireside."

Such was the happy hour of domestic peace and affection that produced one of the most majestic strains in the language, which has been sung in all Christian lands. It is one among many instances on record in which the affectionate confidence of childhood has awakened the sweetest inspiration in the poet's heart, and the most harmonious chords of his lyre.

The hymn as altered reads—

> "Mighty God! while angels bless thee,
> May a sinner praise thy name?"

———

"FAR FROM THE WORLD."

FEW hymns are associated with sweeter and more elevated religious enjoyment than that by Cowper, beginning,

Far from the world, O Lord, I flee,
From strife and tumult far,
From scenes where Satan wages still
His most successful war.

" The calm retreat, the silent shade,
With prayer and praise agree,
And seem by thy sweet bounty made
For those who follow thee."

The occasion of the writing of this hymn is deeply interesting. Cowper had just recovered from a prolonged attack of melancholy, in which his sufferings had been so extreme that he had attempted to take his own life. The storm that had fallen upon him had broken his friendships and divorced his heart from the pleasures of the world. Recovery brought with it a strong desire for the hopes and consolations of a religious life.

During the latter part of his despondency, he had been a patient of good Dr. Cotton, a poet-philanthropist, some of whose best literary productions are yet to be found in choice collections of English literature. Under the judicious advice of this most excellent man, Cowper became a Christian, and began to lead a very devout life. The soothing and controlling influences of religion hastened his recovery, so that he no longer needed the restraints of the Retreat, and Dr. Cotton advised him to leave St. Albans, the scene of his sorrows, and take lodgings in some quiet country town, for retirement.

Cowper went to Huntingdon, a place associated with his best hymns and his most interesting religious experiences. His brother accompanied him thither, and here left him among strangers.

As soon as his brother had departed, the poet felt the solitude of his situation, and his despondency began to return. He wandered forth into the fields ; it was a lovely country, and his spirits began to revive under the influence of the charming rural scenes. His heart was drawn out towards God. Like the disciples on their way to Emmaus, he felt the sweetness of heavenly companionship ; his heart burned within him, and he longed to find a secret place for prayer. He at last came upon a secluded place, overhung by a green bank and shrubbery, and here he knelt down and poured out his soul to God. He felt a renewed sense of his Saviour's presence, and had the sweet assurance that, however his lot might be cast, Providence would direct him aright.

The next day was the Sabbath, and he went to church for the first time since his recovery. The sanctuary seemed new to him, and its services had a spiritual meaning that he had never felt before. The presence of God was on this occasion most gloriously revealed to him.

Not only was his heart changed towards God, but towards the worshippers. Observing a person near him devoutly engaged in worship, he was led to regard him with the deepest affection. He says, "While he [the stranger] was singing psalms I looked at him, and observing him intent on this holy employment, I could not help saying in my heart with much emotion, ' The Lord bless you for praising him whom my soul loveth.'"

After church he immediately went to the solitary place under the mossy bank where he had found so much comfort in praying on the day before, and here again he enjoyed very remarkable spiritual refreshment in prayer. " How," he says, in referring to this occasion, " how shall I express what the Lord did for me, except by saying that he made all his goodness to pass before me? I seemed to speak to him face to face, as a man converseth with his friend. I could say indeed with Jacob, not how dreadful, but how lovely is this place."

"*GOD MOVES IN A MYSTERIOUS WAY.*"

GOD moves in a mysterious way,
  His wonders to perform;
He plants his footstep in the sea,
  And rides upon the storm.

Deep in unfathomable mines
  Of never-failing skill,
He treasures up his bright designs,
  And works his sovereign will.

Ye fearful saints, fresh courage take;
  The clouds ye so much dread
Are big with mercy, and shall break
  In blessings on your head.

Judge not the Lord by feeble sense,
  But trust him for his grace;
Behind a frowning providence
  He hides a smiling face.

His purposes will ripen fast,
  Unfolding every hour:
The bud may have a bitter taste,
  But sweet will be the flower.

Blind unbelief is sure to err,
  And scan his work in vain:
God is his own interpreter,
  And he will make it plain.

This was the last hymn which Cowper contributed to the "Olney Collection," and perhaps the finest and most impressive that he ever wrote. It was composed just before his second attack of insanity; the shadow of the coming eclipse had already touched his mind. It is said that on one occasion Cowper had determined to go to a particular part of the river Ouse and drown himself; that the driver of the post-chaise missed his way, and that the hymn was the result of the mental reaction that followed this evidence of providential protection.

Montgomery says of the hymn, that it is "rendered awfully interesting by the circumstances under which it was written—in the twilight of departing reason."

Though this was the last of Cowper's Olney Hymns, it was not the last hymn that he ever wrote. After the publication of the Olney Hymns, he composed the hymn beginning,

> "To Jesus, the crown of my hope."

This is supposed to have been his last, written as it was amid the departing gleams of religious comfort, before despondency and a sense of spiritual orphanage hopelessly settled upon his mind.

* * *

"*I LOVE TO STEAL AWHILE AWAY.*"

WE read that holy men of old communed with God in deserts and in solitary places, and that the Saviour himself sought the quiet retreats of nature for prayer. Many poets, among them Madame Guyon and Cowper, have sung the beauty of worshipping God in places of rural retirement, where the rocks are altars and the birds are choirs. Madame Guyon herself loved to pray in solitary places, and Cowper but gives his own experience at St. Albans, when he writes the hymn, beginning,

> " Far from the world, O Lord, I flee."

A devotional hymn, found only in old hymn-books, called " The Bower of Prayer," and written by one accustomed to commune with God in the forest, amid the " ivy, the balsam, the wild eglantine," begins,

> " To leave my dear friends and with neighbors to part,
> And go from my own home afflicts not my heart,
> Like the thought of absenting myself for a day
> From that blessed retreat where I 've chosen to pray.

> " The early shrill notes of the loved nightingale
> That sung in the bower I observed as my bell,
> To call me to duty, while birds in the air
> Sung anthems of praise as I went forth to prayer."

The favorite hymn beginning,

> " I love to steal awhile away,"

was written under the promptings of a love of devotion amid rural scenes, and the inflow of a happy Christian experience. Its author was Mrs. Phœbe H. Brown, who was born in Canaan, N. Y., in 1783. It appeared in Nettleton's " Village Hymns," in 1825. The authoress, a devout Christian mother in humble circumstances in life, was accustomed to resort to a solitary place in a wood or grove, toward nightfall, for secret prayer. For this she was severely criticised by a wealthy neighbor, and her feelings in consequence were deeply wounded.

It was a relief to Mrs. Brown to express any strong emotional feeling in poetry, and she made this trial the occasion of writing the hymn so often sung to the music of "Woodstock." The second line as originally written was, "From children and from care."

> I love to steal awhile away
>   From every cumbering care,
> And spend the hours of setting day
>   In humble, grateful prayer.
>
> I love in solitude to shed
>   The penitential tear,
> And all his promises to plead,
>   Where none but God can hear.
>
> I love to think on mercies past,
>   And future good implore,
> And all my cares and sorrows cast
>   On him whom I adore.
>
> I love, by faith, to take a view
>   Of brighter scenes in heaven ;
> The prospect doth my strength renew,
>   While here by tempests driven.
>
> Thus, when life's toilsome day is o'er,
>   May its departing ray
> Be calm as this impressive hour,
>   And lead to endless day.

"WHEN ALL THY MERCIES, O MY GOD.

> When all thy mercies, O my God,
>   My rising soul surveys,
> Transported with the view, I 'm lost
>   In wonder, love and praise.

Oh, how can words with equal warmth
  The gratitude declare
That glows within my ravished heart?
  But thou canst read it there.

To all my weak complaints and cries
  Thy mercy lent an ear,
Ere yet my feeble thoughts had learned
  To form themselves in prayer.

When in the slippery paths of youth
  With heedless steps I ran,
Thine arm, unseen, conveyed me safe,
  And led me up to man.

Through hidden dangers, toils, and deaths,
  It gently cleared my way;
And through the pleasing snares of vice,
  More to be feared than they.

Through every period of my life
  Thy goodness I 'll pursue;
And after death, in distant worlds,
  The pleasing theme renew.

Through all eternity to thee
  A grateful song I 'll raise;
But oh! eternity 's too short
  To utter all thy praise.

The original poem consists of thirteen stanzas, but the part quoted constitutes all of the hymn in common use. The hymn is almost universally familiar.

Addison was made to see clearly God's providential care in his own life and experience. This hymn was inspired by devotional gratitude for his providential escape from shipwreck during a storm off the coast of Genoa.
APPLETON'S ENCYCLOPEDIA.

"O THOU, MY SOUL, FORGET NO MORE."

MOST of our readers are doubtless familiar with Krishnu-Pal's hymn. It is the hymn beginning,

> "O thou, my soul, forget no more
> The Friend who all thy sorrows bore."

But many of them may not know the author as the first Hindoo convert to Christianity.

A writer in a Baptist missionary paper thus relates the story of its origin: Dr. Carey had spent six years of toil in India, and had seen no results from his labors. He had prayed, and studied, and waited with a heavy but not with a despondent heart. At length the Master granted a first token of his favor and blessing. Krishnu, while engaged in his work as a carpenter, fell and broke his arm. Mr. Thomas, Carey's companion and fellow-laborer in the mission, was called to set the broken limb, and after his work as a surgeon was done, he most fervently preached the gospel to the assembled crowd. The unfortunate carpenter was affected even to tears, and readily accepted an invitation to call on the missionaries for further instruction. The truth took deep hold on his heart. He told the story he had heard to his wife and daughter; and they, too, were so much moved that all three offered themselves as candidates for baptism.

While the question of their reception was under discussion, on the 22d of December, 1800, Krishnu and Goluk, his brother, openly renounced their caste and sat down at the table with the missionaries to eat with them. This excited great surprise among the natives. The evening of the same day, Krishnu, his wife and daughter, went before the church, told the process by which they had been led to embrace Christianity, and were received for baptism. The occasion was one of joyful interest. It was, indeed, too full of delicious excitement for Mr. Thomas to bear; for he had been laboring for some seven years as a missionary, and now looked upon his first convert.

When it was reported that Krishnu had thrown up his caste and become a Christian, the wildest excitement prevailed. A mob of two thousand persons gathered around his house. They dragged him and his brother before the magistrate, but could bring no definite charge against them. They were released, and a native soldier placed as a guard at Krishnu's house. When they saw what a wild storm their profession of Christianity had created, the two women faltered and wished to postpone their baptism. Goluk did the same; and Krishnu was left to encounter the odium and withstand the storm alone. He was baptized in the Ganges. The Governor of India, a number of Portuguese, and great crowds of Hindoos and Mohammedans were present to witness the rite. Dr. Carey walked down into the water with his eldest son on one side of him and Krishnu on the other. Amid the profoundest silence he explained that it was not the water of the sacred river that could wash away sin, but the blood of atonement; and then he administered the sacred rite of baptism; breaking down the wall of separation between the Englishman and the Hindoo, and making them brothers in Christ Jesus. All hearts were impressed; the governor wept; and that evening, December 28, for the first time the Lord's Supper was celebrated in Bengalee.

Krishnu was the first of a long line. When he was baptized he was about thirty-six years old; and he lived for more than twenty years a faithful and honored disciple of the Lord. He became an ardent student, and wrote and compiled tracts that were eagerly read by his countrymen. He also wrote a number of hymns. The one we often sing on communion occasions was translated by Dr. Marshman. He died with cholera in 1822, universally lamented.

> O THOU, my soul, forget no more
> The Friend who all thy sorrows bore;
> Let every idol be forgot;
> But, O my soul, forget him not.
>
> Renounce thy works and ways, with grief,
> And fly to this divine relief;
> Nor him forget, who left his throne,
> And for thy life gave up his own.
>
> Eternal truth and mercy shine
> In him, and he himself is thine:
> And canst thou then, with sin beset,
> Such charms, such matchless charms forget?
>
> Oh, no; till life itself depart,
> His name shall cheer and warm my heart;
> And lisping this, from earth I 'll rise,
> And join the chorus of the skies.

"JESUS, MY ALL, TO HEAVEN HAS GONE."

ABOUT the year 1730 there lived in Reading, England, a lad by the name of John Cennick. He had a lively fancy and a warm social nature; he made friends easily, and did not always choose them well, and he allowed himself to be too much influenced by idlers who courted his affection. The age of fifteen did not find him a promising youth; he was fond of cards, novels, and stage-plays, and, but for his warm, susceptible feelings, he might have been classed among the profitless boys of the town.

But he was not happy. His conscience was ever ill at ease, and, as he grew older, he found himself led hither and thither by the mere force of evil associations and habits, while his desultory life lost its charms for him. Solitude constantly presented to his mind the gloomy reflection that the days of youth were swiftly passing, that manhood, too, must soon be gone, and he must die.

One day, while walking the streets of London engaged in serious thought, one of those mental reactions that suddenly arrest a gay life, took away all his relish for worldly pleasures. To use his own language, "While walking hastily in Cheapside, the hand of the Lord touched me, and I at once felt an uncommon fear and dejection." He had often retired to rest with a tortured conscience, but he had never before known a depression of spirit like that. He saw that he was a sinner, that his course was leading to ruin, and that one day he would suffer the penalties of his disregard of the requirements of God. He looked upon the past with regret and the future opened to him no cheering prospect.

This anxious concern continued two years. He daily longed for the peace that religion imparts, and sought for it by reforming his conduct, and by practising self-denial and austerities, but he did not seek it in the love and compassion of Christ. He often fasted till his strength was reduced; he prayed unceasingly, regarding prayer in the light of penance, as an act that would purchase pardon, but the unrest still remained. He had no peace, the great conflict went on in his soul.

One day, while thus sorely tried, and brought almost to the verge of despair, he met with the words, "I AM THY SALVATION." The text was like a revelation to him. It lifted the veil that had long darkened his mind, and he saw the way of peace and safety by casting himself wholly on the mercy of Christ. His mind was filled with unspeakable joy on believing that Jesus would "take him to Him" as he was, with all his imperfections, and pardon all his sin. He now found peace to his soul. The presence of the Saviour seemed continually with him, and he could say, as he afterwards expressed his feelings in verse, in view of the happy change:

> "Thou dear Redeemer, dying Lamb,
>   I love to hear of thee;
> No sound so charming as thy name,
>   Nor half so sweet can be."

He now earnestly entreated his young associates to turn from the pursuit of worldly folly to religion, and the constant theme of his conversation was "peace and pardon through the blood of Christ."

Cennick became a Gospel minister, and was associated with the Wesleys and Whitefield in their labors. He was a fervent-spirited poet, and he thus told in verse the experience we have been relating ; a hymn that all our readers will recognize, though comparatively few may have known the circumstances under which it was written :

> "Jesus, my all, to heaven is gone,
> He whom I fix my hopes upon.
> His path I see, and I 'll pursue
> The narrow way till Him I view.
>
> "The more I strove against his power,
> I felt the weight and guilt the more,
> Till late I heard my Saviour say,
> Come hither, soul, I am the way.
>
> "Lo, glad I come, and thou, blest Lamb,
> Shalt take me to thee as I am.
> Nothing but sin I thee can give,
> Nothing but love shall I receive.
>
> "Now will I tell to sinners round
> What a dear Saviour I have found.
> I 'll point to thy redeeming blood,
> And say, BEHOLD THE WAY TO GOD."

He thus speaks of the same religious experience in one of his poems :

> "Dangers were always in my path,
> And fears of death and endless wrath.
> Though every day I wail my fall
> Three years of grief exceeded all :
> No rest I knew ! a slave of sin,
> With scarce a spark of hope within."

He became a teacher in the school for colliers' children, which Wesley established at Kingswood. In 1745, he severed his connection with the Methodists, and joined the Moravian Brethren. He died at an early age in 1755. His end was peace. After his decease, a poem was found in his pocket, written in anticipation of the final summons, entitled " Nunc Dimittis." The following stanza will show the spirit of resignation in which he viewed the change :

> "O Lamb, I languish
>   Till the day I see
> When thou shalt say,
>   ' Come up and be with Me !'
> Twice seven years
>   Have I thy servant been,
> Now let me end
>   My service and my sin."

"FATHER, WHATE'ER OF EARTHLY BLISS."

THE most unfortunate people are sometimes the most useful. Socrates purblind, Seneca withered, Milton blind, Collins and Cowper distressed with the fear of insanity, Dr. Johnson carrying with him physical and mental infirmity from youth to age, were among the world's benefactors notwithstanding these obstacles to success. From a blighted youth and life-long misfortune have often sprung works of benevolence and sympathy, such as only could result from the discipline of trial.

> " There is a secret in the ways of God
>   With his own children, which none others know,
> That sweetens all he does."

In nearly every collection of hymns, and especially in collections used in Baptist churches, the name of ' Mrs. Steele" is more frequently found than any other female writer. The address "Mrs." is usually placed before her name, though the lady was never married. This usage is common, in England, with maiden ladies entitled to especial respect, and it has been retained by American compilers of devotional poetry and hymns.

She was the daughter of Rev. William Steele, an English Baptist minister in Hampshire. She united with the church under her father's care, and was greatly beloved for her humility, piety, and Christian activities. She was a great sufferer, and from a life of severe discipline grew those sweet Christian graces which find expression in her hymns.

> " Father, whate'er of earthly bliss
>   Thy sovereign will denies,
>   Accepted at thy throne of grace,
>   Let this petition rise :
>
> " Give me a calm and thankful heart,
>   From every murmur free,
>   The blessings of thy love impart,
>   And help me live to Thee."

She met with an accident in childhood which made her an invalid for life. She was also engaged to be married to a gentleman whom she dearly loved, and the preparations were fully made for the wedding. At the very moment when she was expecting the bridegroom's arrival, the guests being already in part assembled, a messenger came with the news that he had just been drowned. Her life, now doubly blighted, sought only consolation in the exercises of piety, charity, and the inspirations of her pen. Her father's death deepened her sorrows in her helpless situation, and weaned her heart from the vanishing things of the world. But she bore her lot in her most shadowed hours with resignation, "looking unto Jesus." Her exit was serene and happy. Wrinkled with sorrow and worn with age, she at last realized a full answer to the burden of her life-long prayer:

> "Let the sweet hope that thou art mine
> My life and death attend;
> Thy presence through my journey shine,
> And crown my journey's end."

Shortly before her departure, she said:

> "I know that my Redeemer liveth."

Her life was told in that hymn. "Earthly bliss" was denied her, but she had a "calm and thankful heart," God's "presence" shone through her "journey," and crowned the "journey's end."

"*JESUS, AND SHALL IT EVER BE!*"

This hymn was written by a pious youth, named Joseph Grigg, when only ten years old. Little is known of his personal history. His early life was passed in humble circumstances. Dr. Joseph Belcher mentions that he continued to exercise his poetical gifts, so early developed. He says: "About half a century ago, we saw a small pamphlet containing nineteen hymns, written by a young man named Grigg, when he was a laboring mechanic." His early piety seems to have had a steady growth and ripe development. He became a Presbyterian minister, and preached for a time in the Presbyterian Chapel, Silver street, London. He died in 1768. The following lines composed on his death by Thomas Green, a local poet, show that his memory was one of those that "smell sweet and blossom in the dust :"

> "Death has, in silence, sealed th' instructive tongue
> That used to captivate the listening throng;
> No more he stands to plead a Saviour's name,
> And these cold hearts of ours with love inflame;
> No more he shows the path where duty lies,
> That path of pleasure leading to the skies."

Grigg's hymn beginning,

> "Jesus, and shall it ever be,"

discovers remarkable maturity of thought for a youth of ten years. It not unfavorably compares with Milton's Psalm, "Let us with a gladsome mind," written at the age of fifteen. The hymn was originally published in five four-line stanzas in the *Gospel Magazine* for April, 1774, under the title,

> "SHAME OF JESUS CONQUERED BY LOVE,
>
> BY A YOUTH OF TEN YEARS."

It was sent to the magazine by Rev. Benjamin Francis, who interested himself in the young Author.

> JESUS, and shall it ever be!
> A mortal man ashamed of thee!
> Scorned be the thought by rich and poor:
> O may I scorn it more and more!
>
> Ashamed of Jesus! sooner far
> Let evening blush to own a star.
> Ashamed of Jesus! just as soon
> Let midnight be ashamed of noon.

C

'T is evening with my soul till He,
That Morning Star bids darkness flee :
He sheds the beams of noon Divine
O'er all this midnight soul of mine.

Ashamed of Jesus ! shall yon field
Blush when it thinks who bid it yield?
Yet blush I must, while I adore,
I blush to think I yield no more.

Ashamed of Jesus ! of that Friend
On whom for heaven my hopes depend?
It must not be ! be this my shame,
That I no more revere his Name.

Ashamed of Jesus ! yes I may ;
When I 've no crimes to wash away ;
No tear to wipe, no joy to crave,
No fears to quell, no soul to save.

Till then, (nor is the boasting vain,)
Till then, I boast a Saviour slain ;
And oh, may this my portion be,
That Saviour not ashamed of me.

"VITAL SPARK OF HEAVENLY FLAME."

THE construction of this funeral anthem and chant is very peculiar, and illustrates how thought may be improved in its expression. (1.) The heathen emperor Adrian, a philosopher as well as a ruler, addressed his soul on his death-bed, in the Latin lines, beginning,

"Animula, blandula, vagula,
    Hospes comesque corporis," etc.

which are familiar to scholars as " Adrian's Address to his Soul when Dying," and which many poets have translated into English verse.   (2.) An old hymn writer by the name of Flatman wrote a Pindaric, somewhat similar to " Adrian's Address," as follows :

> " When on my sick-bed I languish,
> Full of sorrow, full of anguish,
> Fainting, gasping, trembling, crying,
> Panting, groaning, speechless, dying;
> Methinks I hear some gentle spirit say,
> ' Be not fearful, come away.' "

(3.) The poet Pope combined these two poems with the words of Divine inspiration, " O death, where is thy sting? O grave, where is thy victory ?" thus making of the whole a triumphant Christian anthem.

> VITAL spark of heavenly flame,
> Quit, oh quit this mortal frame.
> Trembling, hoping, ling'ring, flying,
> Oh the pain, the bliss of dying!
> Cease, fond nature, cease thy strife,
> And let me languish into life.
>
> Hark! they whisper: angels say,
> " Sister spirit, come away !"
> What is this absorbs me quite,
> Steals my senses, shuts my sight,
> Drowns my spirit, draws my breath,
> Tell me, my soul, can this be death?
>
> The world recedes : it disappears :
> Heaven opens on my eyes ; my ears
>   With sounds seraphic ring.
> Lend, lend your wings ! I mount ! I fly !
> O grave, where is thy victory?
>   O death, where is thy sting?

II. HISTORICAL AND PERSONAL.

6*

HISTORICAL AND PERSONAL.

KING ROBERT SECOND'S HYMN.

Come, thou Holy Spirit, come,
And from thine eternal home
   Shed the ray of light divine;
Come, thou Father of the poor,
Come, thou source of all our store,
   Come, within our bosoms shine.

Thou of Comforters the best,
Thou the soul's most welcome Guest,
   Sweet Refreshment here below!
In our labor Rest most sweet,
Grateful Shadow from the heat,
   Solace in the midst of woe!

Oh, most blessed Light Divine,
Shine within these hearts of thine,
   And our inmost being fill;
If thou take thy grace away,
Nothing pure in man will stay,
   All our good is turned to ill.

Heal our wounds; our strength renew;
On our dryness pour thy dew;
   Wash the stains of guilt away:
Bend the stubborn heart and will,
Melt the frozen, warm the chill,
   Guide the steps that go astray.

> On the faithful, who adore
> And confess thee, evermore
>   In thy sevenfold gifts descend;
> Give them virtue's sure reward,
> Give them thy salvation, Lord,
>   Give them joys that never end.   Amen.

ROBERT II. succeeded Hugh Capet his father, upon the throne of France, about the year 997.   He has been called the gentlest monarch that ever sat upon a throne, and his amiability of character poorly prepared him to cope with his dangerous and wily adversaries.   His last years were embittered by the opposition of his own sons, and the political agitations of the times.   He died at Melun in 1031, and was buried at St. Denis.

Robert possessed a reflective mind, and was fond of learning and musical art.   He was both a poet and a musician.   He was deeply religious, and, from unselfish motives, was much devoted to the church.   He was intimate with Fulbert of Chartres, a man of great learning and religious zeal, of whom Canute and other princes sought advice.

The king and Chartres both produced hymns, which are still used in the English church.   Robert's hymn, "Veni, Sancte Spiritus," is given above.   He himself was a chorister; and there was no kingly service that he seemed to love so well.   We are told that it was his custom to go to the church of St. Dennis, and in his royal robes, with his crown upon his head, to direct the choir at matins and vespers, and join in the singing. Few kings have left a better legacy to the Christian church than his own hymn, which, after nearly a thousand years, is still a tone and an influence in the world.

"St. Fulbert of Chartres' Hymn," which is found in the Church of England's collection, is as follows·

> YE choirs of New Jerusalem,
>   Your sweetest notes employ,
> The Paschal victory to hymn
>   In strains of holy joy.
>
> For Judah's Lion bursts his chains,
>   Crushing the serpent's head;
> And cries aloud, through death's domains
>   To wake the imprisoned dead.
>
> Devouring depths of hell their prey
>   At his command restore;
> His ransomed hosts pursue their way
>   Where Jesus goes before.
>
> Triumphant in his glory now,
>   To him all power is given;
> To him in one communion bow,
>   All saints in earth and heaven.
>
> While we, his soldiers, praise our King,
>   His mercy we implore,
> Within his palace bright to bring
>   And keep us evermore.
>
> All glory to the Father be;
>   All glory to the Son;
> All glory, Holy Ghost, to thee,
>   While endless ages run.

HYMN OF GUSTAVUS ADOLPHUS.

MANY noble hymns were produced in Germany during the Thirty Years' War, but that composed by Altenburg, and known as "Gustavus' Battle Song," is by far the most majestic strain of the period. "As we read the stirring lines, a vision rises before us of two mighty hosts encamped over against each other, stilled by the awe that falls on brave hearts when momentous events are about to be decided. The thick fogs of an autumn morning hide the foes from each other; only the shrill note of the clarion is heard piercing through the mist. Then suddenly in the Swedish camp there is silence. With a solemn mien Gustavus advances to a front rank of his troops, and kneels down in the presence of all of his followers. In a moment the whole army bends with him in prayer. Then there bursts forth the sound of trumpets, and ten thousand voices join in song :"

> FEAR not, O little flock, the foe
> Who madly seeks your overthrow,
> 　　Dread not his rage and power:
> What though your courage sometimes faints,
> His seeming triumph o'er God's saints
> 　　Lasts but a little hour.
>
> Be of good cheer, your cause belongs
> To Him who can avenge your wrongs;
> 　　Leave it to him, our Lord:
> Though hidden yet from all our eyes,
> He sees the Gideon who shall rise
> 　　To save us and his word.

As true as God's own word is true,
Nor earth nor hell with all their crew,
   Against us shall prevail:
A jest and by-word they are grown;
God is with us, we are his own,
   Our victory cannot fail.

Amen, Lord Jesus, grant our prayer!
Great Captain, now thine arm make bare,
   Fight for us once again:
So shall thy saints and martyrs raise
A mighty chorus to thy praise,
   World without end.   Amen.

The army of Gustavus moved forward to victory—an army so inspired with confidence in God could not but be victorious; but at the moment of triumph a riderless horse came flying back to the camp—it was that of the martyred king.

ST. FRANCIS XAVIER'S HYMN.

St. Francis Xavier's hymn has been pronounced, even by Protestant writers, one of the "most profoundly and loftily spiritual" of Christian lyrics, because, as one expresses the leading thought of the composition, "it is the essence of disinterestedness." The following is the original:

O Deus, ego amo Te.
Nec amo Te, ut salves me,
Aut quia non amantes Te
Æterno punis igne.

Tu, Tu, mi Jesu, totum me
Amplexus es in cruce;
Tulisti clavos, lanceam,
Multamque ignominiam,

Innumeros dolores,
Sudores, et angores,
Ac mortem; et hæc propter. me,
Ac pro me peccatore.

Cur igitur non amem Te,
O Jesu amantissime!
Non, ut in cœlo salves me,
Aut in æternum damnes me,

Nec præmii ullius spe,
Sed sicut Tu amasti me;
Sic amo et amabo Te,
Solum, quia Rex meus es.

The hymn purports to be a revelation of the writer's own experience. Francis Xavier was born of a noble family in Spain, in 1506. At the age of sixteen he entered the University of Paris, where he was brought under the influence of Loyola, the celebrated founder of the Order of Jesus. He renounced all worldly ambitions and aims, became a missionary to China, India, and other foreign lands, toiling with a self-forgetful ardor and a self-consuming zeal. He died in the work, in China, in 1552.

My God, I love thee—not because
  I hope for heaven thereby;
Nor yet because who love thee not
  Must burn eternally.

Thou, O my Jesus, thou didst me
  Upon the cross embrace;
For me didst bear the nails and spear,
  And manifold disgrace,

And griefs and torments numberless,
  And sweat of agony,
E'en death itself: and all for me
  Who was thine enemy.

> Then why, O blessed Jesus Christ,
>   Should I not love thee well?
> Not for the sake of winning heaven,
>   Nor of escaping hell;
>
> Not with the hope of gaining aught,
>   Nor seeking a reward,
> But as thyself hast lovéd me,
>   Oh, ever-loving Lord!
>
> E'en so I love thee, and will love,
>   And in thy praise will sing;
> Solely because thou art my God,
>   And my eternal King.

THOMAS A KEMPIS' HYMN.

THE life of Thomas à Kempis was a long solitude, and the known facts of his history are so few that they are easily told. He was born in 1380, in a village near Cologne. His surname was Hammerlein, or little Hammer, translated by the word *Mallcolus* in Latin. Called of God to be a teacher of the experiences of a regenerate inner life, he was of as humble birth as the disciples of Galilee. "He was brought up," says one of his biographers, "in poverty and hardship; his father earned his bread by the sweat of his brow; his mother assiduously watched over the education of her children; she was always attentive to the concerns of the family, abstemious, silent, and extremely modest."

At the age of six he was placed in one of the houses belonging to the "Society of the Brothers and Sisters of Common Life," founded by Gerard de Groote. This was a practical religious order, the members of which devoted themselves to the instruction of youth, and to the cultivation of the mechanic arts. The whole Society had their property in common, but the members made no vow, and were at liberty to resign their places at their own discretion. It was in one of the schools of this Society that Erasmus received his early education.

The particular school in which Thomas à Kempis entered, was in the town of Daventer, in West Friesland, where he was under the instruction of Florentius, the immediate successor of Gerard de Groote. Florentius received him with warm affection into his own family, and gave him many valuable books, the perusal of which was the chief delight of his boyhood. "Much was I pleased," says à Kempis, "with the devout conversation, the irreproachable manners, and the humility of my brethren. I had never seen such piety and charity. They remained constantly at home, employed in prayer and study, or in copying useful books, and sanctifying this occupation by frequent ejaculations of devotion."

A beautiful anecdote is associated with his student history, which illlustrates his elevated piety. His preceptor asked a class of which he was a member, " What passage of Scripture conveys the sweetest description of heaven ?" One answered, " There shall be no more sorrow." Another, " There shall be no more death." Another, "They shall see his face." But Thomas à Kempis, who was the youngest of all, said, " And his servants shall serve Him."

The monks and the religious orders at this period

were the book-makers, and it is through their patient toil that the best literary treasures of the past come down to us. The youth of Thomas à Kempis was spent in copying useful books. "To transcribe works which Jesus Christ loves, by which the knowledge of him is diffused, is a most worthy employment. If *he* shall not lose his reward, who gives a cup of cold water to a thirsty neighbor. what will not be the reward of those, who, by putting good works into the hands of their neighbors, open to them the fountains of eternal life? Blessed are the hands of the transcribers!" Such was his view of the sacredness of his early calling. Not only the classical literature of Greece and Rome, but the precious pages of Holy Writ were transmitted from generation to generation by these useful pens.

At the age of nineteen, Thomas à Kempis, encouraged to pursue the course by his preceptor Florentius, resolved to enter into the Order of the Monks of St. Augustin. "You must not suppose," said Florentius, "that a monastic life can be one of idleness. The good man's prayers must be incessant; his fasts frequent; his sleep short, and the whole of his spare time must be given to manual labor." Upon such a life Thomas à Kempis entered with the freshness of youth yet blooming on his cheek.

The story of his first appearance at the monastery is a pleasing one. It was at the town of Zwoll, on the banks of the Vecht. His brother John à Kempis, whom he had not seen for a long period, was the prior. At the door of the monastery he was met by this brother, who was deeply affected on learning his purpose to become a monk. After the salutation, the two brothers lifted up their voices in devout gratitude, saying :

> " Behold how good
> And how pleasant a thing it is
> For brethren to dwell together in unity.

> " It is like precious ointment upon the head
> That ran down upon the beard,
> Aaron's beard,
> That went down to the skirts of his garments.

> " As the dew of Hermon,
> As the dew that descended upon the mountains of Zion,
> For there the Lord commanded his blessing,
> Even life evermore."

From the time of his vow to his decease, a period of sixty-six years, Thomas à Kempis lived in the monastery of Zwoll. His spiritual enjoyments were at first very great, but they were followed by deep inward conflicts which are described in his " Imitation of Christ." " By degrees," he said, " I was weaned from everything earthly and adhered to God alone. Then I experienced how sweet, how full of mercy God is to those who truly love him." Here he wrote numerous works, among them the lives of his preceptors. He acquired a reputation for uncommon sanctity, and it is said that when he sung in his divine office in the choir, his countenance had a " holy radiance which filled the spectators with awe." But he was very humble, and always refused to entertain those who would do him honor, unless he could give them spiritual help. "I must leave you," he would say to visitors; "there is some one waiting for me in my cell."

Age at last put an end to his activities, and in the long calm twilight of life, he awaited the coming of his Lord. "I have sought for peace everywhere," he said in old age, "but I have found it nowhere except in a corner with a little book." He died on the 25th of July, 1471, in the 92d year of his age.

The following poem, written in ripe experience, expresses his anticipation of heaven:

HEAVEN'S JOYS.

HIGH the angel choirs are raising
  Heart and voice in harmony;
The Creator King still praising
  Whom in beauty there they see.

Sweetest strains from soft harps stealing,
Trumpets' notes of triumph pealing,
Radiant wings and white stoles gleaming
Up the steps of glory streaming;
Where the heavenly bells are ringing;
"Holy! holy! holy!" singing
  To the mighty Trinity!
"Holy! holy! holy!" crying!
For all earthly care and sighing
  In that city cease to be!

Every voice is there harmonious,
Praising God in hymns symphonious;
Love each heart with light unfolding,
As they stand in peace beholding
  There the Triune Deity!

Whom adore the seraphim
　Aye with love eternal burning;
Venerate the cherubim
　To their font of honor turning,
While angelic thrones adoring
　Gaze upon his majesty.

Oh how beautiful that region !
Oh how fair that heavenly legion !
　Human souls and angels blend.
Glorious will that city be,
Full of deep tranquillity,
　Light and peace from end to end !
See the happy dwellers there
　Shine in robes of purity,
　Keep the laws of charity,
Bound in firmest unity;
Labor finds them not, nor care,
　Ignorance can ne'er perplex,
　Nothing tempt them, nothing vex ;
　Joy and health their fadeless blessing'
　Always all good things possessing.

———◆———

SIR WALTER RALEIGH'S HYMN.

FEW of the hymns of the Elizabethan era survive,
though the Ambrosian Midnight Hymn, " Hark, 't is the
Midnight Cry," and the hymns of St. Bernard, and Bernard of Cluny, are still tones in the church, and the religious poetry of Sir Walter Raleigh comes down to us
associated with the history of his brilliant, though sadly
eclipsed career.   The following poem has some fine lines
in the quaint English style of the period, and was com-

posed by Sir Walter Raleigh during his first imprisonment:

MY PILGRIMAGE.

GIVE me my scallop-shell of quiet,
  My staff of faith to walk upon,
My scrip of joy—immortal diet—
  My bottle of salvation,
My gown of glory, hope's true gage—
And thus I take my pilgrimage.

No cause deferred, no vain-spent journey,
For there Christ is the King's attorney,
Who pleads for all without degrees,
And he hath angels, but no fees.
And when the great twelve million jury
Of our sins with direful fury
'Gainst our souls black verdicts give,
Christ pleads his death and then we live.

Be thou my speaker, taintless Pleader,
Unblotted lawyer, true Proceeder:
Thou giv'st salvation even for alms,
Not with a bribéd lawyer's palms ;
And this is my eternal plea,
To him who made heaven, earth and sea.

Blood must be my body's balmer,
While my soul, like faithful palmer,
Travelleth toward the land of heaven ;
Other balm will not be given.

Over the silver mountains
Where spring the nectar fountains,
There will I kiss the bowl of bliss,
And drink my everlasting fill,
Upon every milken hill ;
My soul will be a-dry before,
But after that will thirst no more

Fiftcen years after the composition of this hymn, the brilliant courtier found himself again betrayed by ambition, and again within the prison walls. On the night before his death he wrote the following lines in his Bible, which he left in the little room over the gatehouse, and which were much prized in their day:

> "Even such is time, that takes on trust
>   Our youth, our joy, and all we have,
> And pays us but with earth and dust;
>   Who, in the dark and silent grave,
> When we have wandered all our ways,
> Shuts up the story of our days:
> But from this earth, this grave, this dust,
> My God shall raise me up, I trust."

GERHARDT'S HYMN OF TRUST.

AMONG the sweet strains of poetry which Schiller learned at his mother's knee, were the hymns of that much enduring Lutheran preacher, Paul Gerhardt. The young poet loved them; they filled his mind with spiritual images, and lent an harmonious religious influence to his unformed genius.

The influence was never lost: it lingered like rays of distant splendor amid the speculative mysteries that darkened his declining years, and haunted his dreams, when he saw the sun going down on Weimar, beautiful Weimar, for the last time.

Gerhardt was a great sufferer in the cause of reformed faith, but his sufferings were in a measure compensated by the supports of human love. He was born in Saxony

He became a Christian pastor at the close of the Thirty Years' War, first at a small village called Mittenwalde, and subsequently at Berlin. In 1666, he was deposed from his spiritual office in Berlin on account of his firm adherence to the Lutheran doctrines. He received the reverse submissively, and said with characteristic loftiness of spirit, " I am willing to seal with my blood the evangelical truth, and offer my neck to the sword."

Gerhardt had a lovely and amiable wife, whom he loved with more than ordinary devotion and tenderness. He himself was willing to endure evil speaking, hardship and trial, but it caused him severe pain to think that the burdens of his lot must fall upon her.

A story is told of these altered days, which, although some recent writers have sought to prove it untrustworthy, pious Germans still love to repeat.

He had been ordered to quit the country on account of the difference between his religious sentiments and those of the king. He went in reduced circumstances, with his wife travelling on foot.

One night they came to a village inn. His wife, weary with the journey, and disheartened at her friendless situation, sat down and began to weep. Behind her were the happy scenes of her youth ; before her was a land of strangers.

The poet tried to comfort her, but the tears would flow.

He reminded her of the verse in the Bible: " Commit thy way unto the Lord, trust also in him, and he will bring it to pass." " God will provide," he said. " Commit all of your sorrows into his hands." ·

There was a garden near at hand, and in the garden an arbor. The poet left his weeping wife and went to the arbor for prayer. It was a lovely night in the rosy time of the year. The air was temperate, the sky serene; the moon shimmered on the groves and was glassed on the waters.

The poet's mind was in harmony with nature; he felt a holy calm within, a perfect reliance on God. He began to express his thoughts in verse:

> COMMIT thou all thy griefs
> And ways into His hands;
> To his sure trust and tender care
> Who earth and heaven commands;
> Who points the clouds their course,
> Whom wind and seas obey;
> He shall direct thy wandering feet,
> He shall prepare thy way.
>
> Thou on the Lord rely,
> So, safe, shalt thou go on;
> Fix on his work thy steadfast eye,
> So shall thy work be done.
> No profit canst thou gain
> By self-consuming care;
> To him commend thy cause—his ear
> Attends thy softest prayer.
>
> Give to the winds thy fears;
> Hope, and be undismayed;
> God hears thy sighs and counts thy tears,
> He shall lift up thy head.
> Through waves and clouds and storms
> He gently clears thy way;
> Wait thou his time, so shall this night
> Soon end in joyous day.

He paused for a moment, and thought of his helplessness in a worldly point of view, and of his weeping wife. He then continued :

> Still heavy is thy heart?
>   Still sink thy spirits down?
> Cast off the weight—let fear depart,
>   And every care be gone.
> What though thou rulest not,
>   Yet heaven, and earth, and hell,
> Proclaim—God sitteth on the throne,
>   And ruleth all things well.
>
> Leave to his sovereign sway
>   To choose and to command;
> So shalt thou, wondering, own his way
>   How wise, how strong his hand!
> Far, far above thy thought
>   His counsel shall appear,
> When fully he the work hath wrought
>   That caused thy needless fear.

That night two gentlemen came riding to the inn, and inquired for Paul Gerhardt, the Lutheran preacher and poet.

"I am Paul Gerhardt," said the poet firmly, not knowing what new calamity might follow the confession.

"We have come from Duke Christian," said the men, "who wishes us to express to you his sympathy in your persecutions and afflictions, and to invite you to come to Merseburg, and make that city your home."

"God be praised," said the poet, looking upon the men more in the light of celestial messengers than despatch-bearers from an earthly court. "It is his will."

> "He shall direct thy wandering feet,
> He shall prepare thy way."

Gerhardt thanked the messengers with a heart full of emotion, tears filling his eyes. He went to his room with a beaming countenance, where his poor wife was trying with Christian confidence to restrain her feelings. He told her the news, and handed her the hymn he had written in the garden. "See," he said, "how God provides. Did I not bid you trust in God, and all would be well?"

His wife opened the paper, and her eyes fell upon the poet's words written in the darkest hour of his life, when even her fortitude was giving way to despondency.

> "Commit thou all thy griefs
> And ways into His hands."

Gerhardt died at the age of seventy. His last days were serene, and witnessed to the end the consolations of an all-victorious faith. He was spending the hour in holy exercises, and was in the act of repeating the lines,

> "Death has no power to kill,
> But from many a dreaded ill
> Bears the spirit safe away;"

when the heavenly summons came.

We have said that Schiller loved the hymns of Gerhardt, that he learned them in his boyhood, and that their influence lingered, tinging with a certain spiritual brightness the last poetic dreams of his life. But Schiller's faith was not clear. He, too, died repeating poetry, but not, like Gerhardt, with a triumphant expression of

Christian confidence, but, like his own religious life, now gloomed, now shining, a poem of hope mingled with doubt and uncertainty:

> " From out this dim and gloomy hollow,
>   Where hang the cold clouds heavily,
> Could I but gain the clew to follow,
>   How blessed would that journey be.
>
> " Aloft I see a fair dominion,
>   Through time and change all vernal still,
> But what the power, and where the pinion,
>   To gain that ever-blooming hill?
>
> " For lo! between us rolls a river,
>   O'er which a wrathful tempest raves;
> I feel the spirit shrink and shiver
>   To gaze upon its gloomy waves!"

The heavenly way, which, to Gerhardt, was one of excessive brightness, had a shadow for Schiller, even in life's sunset, but he still aspired for the religious faith of the great master of German sacred song.

Another hymn by Gerhardt has many translations:

> QUIETLY rest the woods and dales,
> Silence around the earth prevails,
>   The world is all asleep:
> Then, my soul, in thought arise,
> Seek thy·Father in the skies,
>   And holy vigils keep.
>
> Now my body seeks for rest,
> From its vestments all undressed,
>   Types of immortality:
> Christ shall give me soon to wear
> Garments beautiful and fair,
>   White robes of majesty.

Weary limbs now rest ye here,
Safe from danger and from fear,
      Seek slumber on this bed—
Deeper rest ere long to share :
Other hands shall soon prepare
      My couch among the dead.

While my eyes I gently close,
Stealing o'er me soft repose,
      Who shall now my guardian be ?
Soul and body now I leave,
And thou wilt the trust receive,
      Israel's Watchman, unto thee.

This is the favorite evening hymn in Germany. The same thoughts are expressed in Elder John Leland's evening hymn, beginning,

" The day has passed and gone,
      The evening shades appear;
Oh, may we all remember well
      The night of death draws near.

" We lay our garments by,
      Upon our beds to rest;
So death will soon disrobe us all
      Of what we here possess."

----•----

KLOPSTOCK'S HYMN.

IN an old churchyard in Ottensen, near the venerable city of Hamburgh, stood a memorial stone, around which groups of thoughtful people used to gather in the soft twilights of the golden summer days. It marked the grave of a lady, famous both as the wife of an admired

Christian poet, and as a model of intellectual loveliness and of simple, trustful religious faith. At the top of the antique memorial were carved two sheaves of wheat, one leaning on the other, and beneath the touching emblem was inscribed :

" Seed sown by God,
To ripen in the day of harvest.

MARGARETTA KLOPSTOCK

Waits where death is not, for her friend, her lover, her husband, whom she so much loves, and by whom she is so much beloved. But we shall rise from this grave, thou, my Klopstock, and I, and our son, for whom I died, to worship Him, who died, and was buried, and is risen."

Margaretta Moller was born March 19, 1728. She was the daughter of a Hamburgh merchant, and she received a liberal education. She possessed great beauty of mind and of character even in girlhood. Her æsthetic tastes predominated ; her thoughts were tinged with poetic fancy, and her heart was a pure fountain ever brimming with love. She was a pious maiden, and her dispositions were attuned in perfect harmony by the sweet influences of prayer.

When verging on womanhood, she became enamored of the poetry of Klopstock. The *Messiah*, as far as it was written, was passing through rapid editions, and the German Milton was in the zenith of his sudden and re-splendent fame. He was a stranger to Margaretta Moller : she had never met with him, nor seen him, but she begun to take a mysterious interest in his history, and to find loving companionship in the creations of his muse. No music was so sweet to her as his mellifluous hexameters. As she dwelt on his sublime flights of seraph-like song, and caught new light from his luminous spirit, her affections began to be engaged in one whom she never saw, nor ever expected to see. She wrote in a letter to a friend : " In one happy night I read my husband's poem the *Messiah.* I was extremely touched with it. The next day I asked one of his friends who was the author of this poem ; and this was the first time I heard Klopstock's name."

In 1751, Klopstock, having received an invitation from Frederick V. to visit the Danish court, set out for Copenhagen, and on his journey stopped at Hamburgh. He was informed of the interest that Miss Moller took in his poetry, and learning something of her elegant taste and excellence of character, he made her a visit. Lavater, who was an enthusiastic admirer of the *Messiah,* calls Klopstock " that confidant of the angels." He was indeed a most humble and exemplary man, and there were times of poetic inspiration, when his pure spirit seemed to gleam with seraphic fire. He united a masculine genius to a womanly tenderness of thought and feeling, and in disposition and tastes, he was a perfect counterpart of Margaretta Moller. The meeting of these congenial spirits could hardly fail to enkindle a flame of pure, trustful love. Klopstock went to the splendors of the Danish court, enamored of Meta, and Miss Moller declared after his departure that her thoughts were all of Klopstock. A correspondence followed, and in a year he again visited Hamburgh, when the happy lovers were betrothed. Two years afterwards they were married.

The married life of Klopstock presents a scene of connubial felicity that seems more like a dream of romance than sober reality. Accounts of it have been published in many tongues, and have added much to the high esteem in which he ever has been held as a Christian and a man. She speaks of the union in her girlish way, in a letter, written not long before her decease: "We married, and I am the happiest wife in the world."

The last cantos of the *Messiah* owe much of their peculiar beauty to the inspiration that Meta afforded the charming poet. In a letter dated Hamburgh, May 6, 1758, she thus pictures the halcyon days of their literary life :

"It will be a delightful occupation for me, to make you more acquainted with my husband's poem. Nobody can do it better than I, being the person that knows the most of that which is not yet published ; being always present at the birth of the young verses, which begin always by fragments here and there, of a subject of which his soul is just then filled. He has many great fragments of the whole work ready. You may think that persons who love as we do have no need of two apartments ; we are always in the same. I with my little work, still— still—only regarding sometimes my husband's sweet face, which is so venerable at that time ! with tears of devotion, and all the sublimity of the subject, my husband reading me his young verses and suffering my criticisms. Ten books are published, which I think probably the middle of the whole."

In the autumn of 1758, she was about to become a

mother. Her joy in prospect of the event is expressed in many delightful and exquisitely delicate passages in her correspondence. The union of the wedded pair never had been so spiritual and sympathetic as in these serene autumn days. Each lived for the happiness of the other, and both dwelt in the perpetual sunlight of God.

But the light of Paradise was glimmering amid the sunbeams of these happy days. Meta Klopstock was treading the borders of the unseen world. After the birth of her child, her health sunk rapidly, and it became evident that her life was drawing to a close.

Her death scene is one of the most beautiful in biography, and, perhaps, no one has touched upon it more tenderly than the great poet himself. He thus describes one of their last affecting interviews : " I came in just as she had been bled. A light having been brought near, I saw her face clearly for the first time after many hours. Ah, my Cramer, the hue of death was on it. But that God who was so mightily with her supported me too at the sight. I said, 'I will fulfil my promise, my Meta, and tell you that your life, from extreme weakness, is in danger.' I pronounced over her the name of the Father, the Son, and the Holy Ghost. 'Now the will of Him who inexpressibly supports thee, his will be done !' 'Let him do according to his will,' said she ; 'He will do well.' She said this is a most sweet, expressive tone of joy and confidence. 'You have endured like an angel ; God has been with you ; he will be with you. His mighty name be praised. The Most Merciful will support you.' 'Be my guardian angel, if our God permit.' 'Who would not be

so ?' said she.   At parting she said to me very sweetly,
'Thou wilt follow me.'

"Shortly after her release, I wished to see what I
had just before called my Meta.   They prevented me.
I said to one of our friends, 'Then I will forbear.   *She
will rise again.'*"

The great poet yielded to no weak repinings in these
altered days.   Heaven to him brightened with new attractions, and his soul was filled with ineffable delight in
his religious contemplations and devotions.   Of one of
these seasons of spiritual elevation he writes :

"The second night came the blessing of her death.
Till then I had looked upon it only as a trial.   The
blessing of such a death in its full power came on me.
I passed above an hour in silent rapture.   The highest
degree of peace with which I am acquainted was in my soul.

"It is impossible to describe all the blessings of that
hour.   I was never before with such certainty convinced
of my salvation."

Happy soul ! Of himself he could say in the hour of
his desolation, "I know that my Redeemer liveth," and
of Meta, "She will rise again."

THOU SHALT RISE.

FROM THE GERMAN OF KLOPSTOCK.

Thou shalt rise ! my dust, thou shalt arise !
Not always closed thine eyes :
   Thy life's first Giver
   Will give thee life for ever,
      Ah ! praise his name !

Sown in darkness, but to bloom again.
When, after winter's reign,
    Jesus is reaping
    The seed now quietly sleeping.
        Ah! praise his name!

Day of praise! for thee thou wondrous day,
In my quiet grave I stay;
    And when I number
    My days and nights of slumber,
        Thou wakest me!

Then, as they who dream, we shall arise
With Jesus to the skies,
    And find that morrow,
    The weary pilgrim's sorrow
        All past and gone!

Then, with the Holiest I tread,
By my Redeemer led,
    Through heaven soaring,
    His holy name adoring
        Eternally!

———+———

SAMUEL RUTHERFORD.

The expression

> "But glory, glory dwelleth
> In Immanuel's land,"

has been often quoted, and the hymn to which these lines are the refrain has come into general use. The hymn as printed in the hymn-books is but a fragment of a long poem. It has a beautiful origin and an interesting history.

Samuel Rutherford was a Scotch divine at Anworth,

and because of his fidelity to the doctrines of the reformed faith, was immured in the dungeons of St Andrew.

> "For Anworth was not heaven,
>   And preaching was not Christ."

He remained true to his convictions of duty to the last, and died in triumph. His last words were: "Glory, glory dwelleth in Immanuel's land!" This expression forms the refrain of the following very tender religious ballad, which we reproduce entire:

THE sands of time are sinking,
  The dawn of heaven breaks,
The summer morn I 've sighed for—
  The fair, sweet morn—awakes.
Dark, dark hath been the midnight,
  But dayspring is at hand;
And glory, glory dwelleth
  In Immanuel's land.

Oh! well it is for ever—
  Oh! well for evermore:
My nest hung in no forest
  Of all this death-doomed shore;
Yea, let this vain world vanish,
  As from the ship the strand,
While glory, glory dwelleth
  In Immanuel's land.

There the red Rose of Sharon
  Unfolds its heartsome bloom,
And fills the air of heaven
  With ravishing perfume;
Oh! to behold it blossom,
  While by its fragrance fanned,
Where glory, glory dwelleth,
  In Immanuel's land!

The King there, in his beauty,
  Without a veil is seen ;
" It were a well-spent journey,
  Though seven deaths lay between."
The Lamb with his fair army
  Doth on Mount Zion stand,
And glory, glory dwelleth
  In Immanuel's land.

O Christ—He is the fountain,
  The deep, sweet well of love !
The streams on earth I 've tasted,
  More deep I 'll drink above :
There to an ocean fulness
  His mercy doth expand,
And glory, glory dwelleth
  In Immanuel's land.

Oft in yon sea-beat prison
  My Lord and I held tryst ;
For Anworth was not heaven,
  And preaching was not Christ.
And aye my murkiest storm-cloud
  Was by a rainbow spanned,
Caught from the glory dwelling
  In Immanuel's land.

But that he built a heaven
  Of his surpassing love—
A little New Jerusalem
  Like to the one above—
" Lord, take me o'er the water,"
  Had been my loud demand ;
" Take me to love's own country
  Unto Immanuel's land !"

But flowers need night's cool darkness,
  The moonlight, and the dew;
So Christ, from one who loved it,
  His shining oft withdrew.
And then for cause of absence
  My troubled soul I scanned;
But glory *shadeless* shineth
  In Immanuel's land.

The little birds of Anworth—
  I used to count them blest;
Now beside happier altars
  I go to build my nest;
O'er these there broods no silence,
  No graves around them stand:
For glory deathless dwelleth
  In Immanuel's land.

Fair Anworth by the Solway,
  To me thou still art dear;
E'en from the verge of heaven
  I drop for thee a tear.
Oh, if one soul from Anworth
  Meet me at God's right hand,
My heaven will be *two* heavens,
  In Immanuel's land.

I 've wrestled on toward heaven,
  'Gainst storm, and wind, and tide;
Now, like a weary traveller
  That leaneth on his guide,
Amid the shades of evening,
  While sinks life's lingering sand,
I hail the glory dawning
  From Immanuel's land.

Deep waters crossed life's pathway,
  The hedge of thorns was sharp ;
Now these lie all behind me.
  Oh, for a well tuned harp !
Oh, to join Hallelujah
  With yon triumphant band,
Who sing where glory dwelleth,
  In Immanuel's land !

With mercy and with judgment
  My web of time he wove,
And aye the dews of sorrow
  Were lustered with his love.
I 'll bless the hand that guided,
  I 'll bless the heart that planned,
When throned where glory dwelleth,
  In Immanuel's land.

Soon shall the cup of glory
  Wash down earth's bitterest woes ;
Soon shall the desert brier
  Break into Eden's rose ;
The curse shall change to blessing,
  The name on earth that 's banned
Be graven on the White Stone
  In Immanuel's land.

Oh, I am my Belovéd's,
  And my Beloved is mine !
He brings a poor vile sinner
  Into his "house of wine."
I stand upon his merit;
  I know no safer stand,
Not even where glory dwelleth,
  In Immanuel's land.

I shall sleep sound in Jesus,
  Filled with his likeness rise,
To love and to adore him,
  To see him with these eyes;
'Tween me and resurrection
  But Paradise doth stand,
Then—then for glory, dwelling
  In Immanuel's land!

The bride eyes not her garments,
  But her dear bridegroom's face:
I will not gaze at glory,
  But at my King of grace;
Not at the crown he giveth,
  But on his piercèd hand:
The Lamb is all the glory
  Of Immanuel's land.

I have borne scorn and hatred,
  I have borne wrong and shame,
Earth's proud ones have reproached me
  For Christ's thrice blessèd name.
Where God's seal's set the fairest,
  They 've stamped their foulest brand;
But judgment shines like noonday
  In Immanuel's land.

They 've summoned me before them,
  But there I may not come;
My Lord says, " Come up hither;"
  My Lord says, " Welcome home;"
My King at his white throne
  My presence doth command,
Where glory, glory dwelleth,
  In Immanuel's land.

ADDISON'S TRAVELLER'S HYMN.

How are thy servants blessed, O Lord,
    How sure is their defence !
Eternal Wisdom is their guide,
    Their help Omnipotence.

In foreign realms, and lands remote,
    Supported by thy care,
Through burning climes they pass unhurt,
    And breathe in tainted air.

When by the dreadful tempest borne
    High on the broken wave,
They know thou art not slow to hear,
    Nor impotent to save.

The storm is laid, the winds retire,
    Obedient to thy will ;
The sea, that roars at thy command,
    At thy command is still.

In midst of dangers, fears, and deaths,
    Thy goodness we 'll adore ;
We 'll praise thee for thy mercies past,
  . And humbly hope for more.

Our life, while thou preserv'st that life,
    Thy sacrifice shall be :
And death, when death shall be our lot,
    Shall join our souls to thee.

This hymn, often used in divine worship by travellers,
was first published in No. 489 of the " Spectator," for
Sept. 20, 1712. The article to which it is appended is
on the sublimity of the sea, and the passages that describe the majestic phenomena of the deep in Holy
Writ. It was doubtless written while the ocean scenery

was fresh in the author's mind, and is a choice expression of a peculiar Christian experience. It is claimed that Addison wrote this piece immediately after his continental tour in 1700–1. The original has a fine stanza that is commonly omitted:

> " Thy mercy sweetened every soil,
>   Made every region please,
> The hoary Alpine hills it warmed,
>   And smoothed the Tyrrhene seas."

COUNT ZINZENDORF'S HYMN.

J. WESLEY'S TRANSLATION.

JESUS, thy blood and righteousness
My beauty are, my glorious dress:
'Midst flaming worlds, in these arrayed,
With joy shall I lift up my head.

Bold shall I stand in thy great day,
For who aught to my charge shall lay?
Fully absolved through these I am—
From sin and fear, from guilt and shame.

The holy, meek, unspotted Lamb,
Who from the Father's bosom came—
Who died for me, e'en me t' atone—
Now for my Lord and God I own.

Lord, I believe thy precious blood—
Which, at the mercy-seat of God
For ever doth for sinners plead—
For me, e'en for my soul, was shed.

Lord, I believe were sinners more
Than sands upon the ocean shore,
Thou hast for all a ransom paid,
For all a full atonement made.

> When from the dust of death I rise
> To claim my mansion in the skies,
> E'en then shall this be all my plea,
> Jesus hath lived and died for me.

The first stanza of the above hymn is very well known in Germany, and is there frequently quoted at deathbeds, as Dr. Watts' stanza, beginning,

> "Jesus can make a dying bed,'

is quoted in the English tongue. The sentiment in the fourth and fifth stanzas was particularly acceptable to the primitive Methodists.

The hymn, which in the original has thirty stanzas, was written by Count Zinzendorf, (1700–1760,) one of the purest and most spiritual of men, the founder of the religious community of Herrnhut, and the champion and defender of the United Moravian Brethren.

His childhood was remarkable for its confiding simplicity and the beauty of piety. He used to gather children to pray with him, and his pure and aspiring imagination found delight in writing messáges of love to the Saviour. Referring to his youthful days and the purity of his motives, he says: "The desire to bring souls to Jesus took possession of me, and my heart became fixed on the Lamb."

From his eleventh to his sixteenth year, Zinzendorf studied at Halle, under the pietist Franke, the founder of the celebrated orphan school. He travelled widely, obtained great learning, and a large knowledge of society. He became in early life enamored of Theodosia, the daughter of the Countess of Castell, but from a

strong sense of duty, resigned his place in her heart to the reigning Count of Reussebersdorf. "From that moment," he said to Charles Wesley, of this act of self-sacrifice, "I was freed from all self-seeking, so that for ten years I have not done my own will in anything, great or small. My own will is hell to me."

In 1731 Count Zinzendorf resigned all public duties, and the encumbrances that follow rank, to devote himself to the service of the Moravian Brethren. He travelled extensively in their behalf, extending his journeys to America, where he labored more than a year in Pennsylvania. He wrote many works, and two thousand hymns. Among his last words were, "I am going to my Saviour."

His hymn, beginning,

> "Jesus, thy blood and righteousness,"

was written on the island of St. Eustatius, on his return from visiting the missionaries in the West Indies. He was filled at the time with a large missionary spirit, and a lofty religious confidence, as the hymn itself strongly evidences.

LADY HUNTINGDON'S HYMN.

SELINA, Countess of Huntingdon, the friend of Whitefield, devoted her time and fortune to the welfare of others. In her maidenhood she heard her sister-in-law, Lady Margaret Hastings, remark, that since she had known and believed in the Lord Jesus Christ for life and salvation, she had been as happy as an angel.

This remark made an impression upon her mind. It

led her to desire to become a follower of Christ, and after-wards resulted in her belief in him as her Saviour. Her after-life was very attractive in the devoted piety that she exhibited by her unwearied usefulness. She erected chapels at her own expense, and lived abstemiously that she might give more money to the poor and advance the religion of her Master.

Her religious experience was continuous, and was sanctified by affliction :

> " The world can neither give, nor take,
>   Nor can they comprehend
> The peace of God, which Christ has bought—
>   The peace which knows no end.
>
> " The burning bush was not consumed,
>   While God remainéd there ;
> The three, when Jesus made the Fourth,
>   Found fire as soft as air.
>
> " God's furnace doth in Zion stand,
>   But Zion's God sits by,
> As the refiner views his gold,
>   With an observant eye.
>
> " His thoughts are high, his love is wise,
>   His wounds a cure intend ;
> And, though he does not always smile,
>   He loves unto the end."

She died at the age of eighty-four. A year before her death she met with an accident, which was the beginning of her last illness. Although in great pain, her mind was at perfect peace. As death drew near, she often said, with emphasis, "The coming of the Lord draweth nigh! The thought fills me with joy unspeakable!"

Here was the ground of her hopes and her happiness: "I see," she said, "myself a poor worm, drawing near to Jesus. What hope could I entertain if I did not know the efficacy of his blood? How little could anything that I have done give a moment's rest at such an hour as this! I confess I have no hope but that which inspired the dying malefactor at the side of my Lord, and I must be saved in the same way, as freely, as fully, or not at all."

New views and revelations came to her in her triumph over the terrors of death. "I cannot tell you," she said, "in what light I now see these words: 'If a man love me, he will keep my words, and my Father will love him, and we will come unto him, and make our abode with him.' To have in this room such company, and to have such an eternal prospect! I see this subject now in a light impossible to be described. I know my capacity will be then enlarged, but I am now as sensible of the presence of God, as I am of the presence of those I have with me."

Her dying testimony was a fitting close to so grand an earthly life.

"My work is done; I have nothing to do but to go to my Father!"

Lady Huntingdon's motives were very pure and sincere, and she ruled her life by secret self-examination, living always with eternity in view. Her best known hymn has reference to this constant aim to keep a blameless conscience in the sight of God.

WHEN thou, my righteous Judge, shalt come,
To take thy ransomed people home,
    Shall I among them stand?
Shall such a worthless worm as I,
Who sometimes am afraid to die,
    Be found at thy right hand?

I love to meet thy people now,
Before thy feet with them to bow,
    Though vilest of them all;
But can I bear the piercing thought
What if my name should be left out,
    When thou for them shalt call?

O Lord, prevent it by thy grace:
Be thou my only hiding place,
    In this th' accepted day;
Thy pardoning voice oh let me hear,
To still my unbelieving fear,
    Nor let me fall, I pray.

Among thy saints let me be found,
Whene'er the archangel's trump shall sound,
    To see thy smiling face;
Then loudest of the throng I 'll sing,
While heaven's resounding arches ring
    With shouts of sovereign grace.

JOHN WESLEY'S HYMN.

How happy is the pilgrim's lot:
How free from every anxious thought,
    From worldly hope and fear!
Confined to neither court nor cell,
His soul disdains on earth to dwell,
    He only sojourns here.

This happiness in part is mine,
Already saved from low design,
  From every creature-love;
Blest with the scorn of finite good,
My soul is lightened of its load,
  And seeks the things above.

The things eternal I pursue,
My happiness beyond the view
  Of those who basely pant;
The things by nature felt and seen,
Their honors, wealth, and pleasures **mean,**
  I neither have nor want.

There is my house and portion fair;
My treasure and my heart are there,
  And my abiding home;
For me my elder brethren stay,
And angels beckon me away,
  And Jesus bids me come.

I come, thy servant, Lord, replies;
I come to meet thee in the skies,
  And claim my heavenly rest!
Soon will the pilgrim's journey end;
Then, O my Saviour, Brother, Friend,
  Receive me to thy breast!

This hymn, which we give as we find it in many collections, but which is greatly extended by the narration of personal circumstances in the original, was written by John Wesley, at the most stormy and tempestuous period of his life, when his lot from a worldly point of view would have been deemed anything but happy.

On February 17, 1746, when days were short and weather far from favorable, he set out on horseback from

Bristol to Newcastle, a distance between three and four hundred miles. The journey occupied ten weary days. Brooks were swollen, and in some places the roads were impassable, obliging the itinerant to go round through the fields. At Aldrige Heath, in Straffordshire, the rain turned to snow, which the northerly wind drove against him, and by which he was soon crusted over from head to foot. At Leeds, the mob followed him, and pelted him with whatever came to hand. He arrived at Newcastle, February 26, "free from every anxious thought," and "every worldly fear."

It was amid such scenes as these that the hymn was written, though we have not the exact date.

The hymn in the original is autobiographical. Wesley had at the time of writing it no wife, and he held no property, having made over his estates to trustees. He says,

> " I have no babes to hold me here,
>   But children more sincerely dear
>   Than mine I humbly claim,
>   Better than daughters or than sons,
>   Temples divine of living stones,
>   Inscribed in Jesus' name.

> " No foot of land do I possess,
>   No cottage in the wilderness ;
>   A poor wayfaring man,
>   I lodge awhile in tents below,
>   Or gladly wander to and fro,
>   Till I my Canaan gain."

John Wesley was disposed to lightly regard all of the scenes of distressing self-sacrifice associated with his itinerant labors.   After a most calamitous journey, he once was known to declare :

> "Pain, disappointment, sickness, strife,
> Whate'er molests or troubles life,
> When past, as nothing we esteem,
> And pain like pleasure is a dream."

CHARLES WESLEY'S WATCH-NIGHT HYMNS.

WESLEY concluded the eventful year of 1740 at Bristol, by holding a watch-meeting, proposed by James Rogers, a Kingswood collier, noted among his neighbors for his playing on the violin, but who, being awakened under the ministry of Charles Wesley, went home, burnt his fiddle, and told his wife he meant to seek religion.

This was the first watch-night meeting among the Methodists.   The people met at half-past eight: the house was filled from end to end, and " we concluded the year," says Wesley, "wrestling with God in prayer, and praising him for the wonderful work which he had already wrought upon the earth."

The meeting became a favorite one and was held monthly.   The church in ancient times was accustomed to spend whole nights in prayer, which nights were termed *vigiliæ* or vigils : and sanctioned by such authority, Wesley appointed monthly watch-nights, on the Friday nearest the full moon, desiring that they, and they only should attend, who could do so without prejudice to their business or families.

The annual watch-night services on New Year's eves,

appointed by the Wesleys, had been continued by the Wesleyan societies. Charles Wesley wrote, both for the monthly watch-night, and for the annual watch-night, a number of hymns whose sublime and solemn language is in harmony with the impressive and somewhat poetic occasions that inspired them. One of these begins, " Ye virgin souls, arise."

Another :

> How many pass the guilty night,
>   In revelling and frantic mirth !
> The creature is their sole delight—
>   Their happiness the things of earth :
> For us suffice the season past :
> We choose the better part at last.
>
> We will not close our wakeful eyes,
>   We will not let our eyelids sleep,
> But humbly lift them to the skies,
>   And all a solemn vigil keep ;
> So many nights on sin bestowed,
> Can we not watch one hour for God ?

WATCH-NIGHT.

> How happy, gracious Lord, are we,
> Divinely drawn to follow thee,
>   Whose hours divided are
> Betwixt the mount and multitude :
> Our day is spent in doing good,
>   Our night in praise and prayer.
>
> With us no melancholy void,
> No moment lingers unemployed
>   Or unimproved below :
> Our weariness of life is gone,
> Who lived to serve our God alone,
>   And only thee to know.

The winter's night and summer's day
Glide imperceptibly away,
  Too short to sing thy praise;
Too few we find the happy hours,
And haste to join those heavenly bowers
  In everlasting lays.

With all who chant thy name on high,
And, Holy, holy, holy! cry,
  (A bright, harmonious throng)
We long thy praises to repeat,
And ceaseless sing around thy seat
  The new eternal song.

NEW YEAR'S VIGIL.

Come, let us anew our journey pursue,
  Roll round with the year,
And never stand still till the Master appear.
His adorable will let us gladly fulfil,
  And our talents improve,
By the patience of hope, and the labor of love.

Our life is a dream; our time, as a stream,
  Glides swiftly away,
And the fugitive moment refuses to stay.
The arrow is flown—the moment is gone;
  The millennial year
Rushes on to our view, and eternity 's here.

O that each, in the day of his coming, may say—
  I have fought my way through:
I have finished the work thou didst give me to do.
Oh that each from his Lord may receive the glad word—
  Well and faithfully done!
Enter into my joy, and sit down on my throne.

CHARLES WESLEY'S HYMN IN TIME OF TROUBLE.

EARLY in the year 1750, the city of London was twice severely shaken by shocks of an earthquake. Several weeks elapsed between the first and second convulsions, during which interim, the earth seems to have been internally agitated. The public mind was unsettled with apprehension, and the parks and squares, where the people were wont to assemble, presented at times a very impressive spectacle.

For several years after the threatened calamity at London, the earth seemed to be in trouble. The stroke came at last, but it fell upon the South, upon Lisbon and Quito. The work of destruction in these two cities indicates the magnitude of the calamity to which the great centre of life on the eastern isle seemed to be exposed.

George Whitefield and Charles Wesley were in London during these days of peril. Seldom, if ever, had these zealous men preached so acceptably as they did then. The most profane were overawed by the danger and sublimity of the situation, and the most hardened and unbelieving were eager to listen to the doctrine of God's providence, and to the promises of the gospel. Mr. Whitefield once preached a sermon at midnight to an immense concourse of people in Hyde Park, who seemed to receive the truth as from the very brink of eternity. The effect was impressive in the extreme. Cries and groans were heard on every hand. Penitent ejaculations and prayers for mercy trembled on every lip.

The following extracts from a letter, written at London at this time, afford a brief but interesting view of the agitated city :

" All London has been, for some days past, under terrible apprehensions of another earthquake. Yesterday thousands fled from the town, it having been confidently predicted by a dragoon that he had a revelation that a great part of the city, and Westminster especially, would be destroyed by an earthquake on the 4th instant, between twelve and one at night. The whole city was under direful apprehensions. Places of worship were crowded with frightened sinners, especially our two chapels, and the tabernacle, where Mr. Whitefield preached. Several of the classes came to their leaders, and desired that they would spend the night with them in prayer ; which was done, and God gave them a blessing. Indeed all around was awful. Being not at all convinced of the prophet's mission, and having no call from any of my brethren, I went to bed at my usual time, believing I was safe in the hands of Christ; and likewise, that, by doing so, I should be the more ready to rise to the preaching in the morning ; which I did, praise be to my kind protector.

* * * * * * * * *

" Though crowds left the town on Wednesday night, yet crowds were left behind ; multitudes of whom, for fear of being suddenly overwhelmed, left their houses, and repaired to the fields, and open places in the city. Tower Hill, Moorfields, but above all, Hyde Park, were filled the best part of the night, with men, women, and children, lamenting. Some, with stronger imaginations than others, mostly women, ran crying in the streets, ' An earthquake! an earthquake !' Such distress, perhaps, is not recorded to have happened before in this careless city. Mr. Whitefield preached at midnight in Hyde Park. Surely God will visit this city ; it will be a time of mercy to some. Oh may I be found watching !"

An incident occurred at this time which we have frequently called to mind as a very impressive illustration of what is termed the majesty of faith. The second shock of the earthquake occurred on the morning of the 8th of March. At an early hour, Rev. Charles Wesley appeared before a great audience who had assembled at the foundry to listen to a morning discourse. He was about to begin his sermon, when a subterranean thundering was heard and the whole city began to shake and totter. The foundry reeled to and fro and seemed every moment about to fall. The worshippers shrieked, and each one felt that his hour had come. The soul of the preacher at this critical juncture seemed touched with an inspiration as from on high. With a face glowing with triumph, and an eye flashing as with ethereal fire, he raised his hands and uttered the sublime language of the Psalmist : " Therefore we will not fear, though the earth be removed, and the mountains be carried into the midst of the sea. The Lord of hosts is with us, the God of Jacob is our refuge !"

The entry in his journal for that date was as follows :

"March 8, 1750. This morning, a quarter after five, we had another shock of an earthquake far more violent than that of February 8. I was just repeating my text, when it shook the foundry so violently, that we all expected it to fall on our heads. A great cry followed from the women and children. I immediately called out, 'Therefore we will not fear, though the earth be moved, and the mountains be carried into the midst of the sea. The Lord of hosts is with us, the God of Jacob is our refuge.' He filled my heart with faith, and my mouth with words, shaking their souls as well as their bodies. The earth moved westward, then eastward, then westward again, through all London and Westminster. It was a strong and jarring motion, attended with a rumbling noise like that of thunder."

The faith that could stand unmoved at such an hour would triumph amid the wreck of matter and the crush of worlds.

This anecdote of the zealous preacher seems to us interesting for the information it imparts. It gives us a certain feeling of confidence when singing the lyrics of Dr. Watts, to recall that he himself felt all of those sweet consolations of which he so fervently wrote. Charles Wesley composed very numerous hymns on the triumphs of faith, a number of which are to be found in almost every work of psalmody. It is edifying to know that he himself was an example of that all-conquering faith to which he devoted his pen.

He thus alludes to the events we have described in some lines written in 1755.

10*

How happy are the little flock,
Who, safe beneath their guardian-rock
  In all commotions rest !
When war's and tumult's waves run high,
Unmoved, above the storm they lie,
  They lodge in Jesus' breast.

The plague, the dearth, the din of war,
Our Saviour's swift approach declare,
  And bid our hearts arise ;
Earth's basis shook confirms our hope ;
Its cities' fall but lifts us up
  To meet him in the skies.

The tokens we with joy confess :
The war proclaims the Prince of Peace,
  The earthquake speaks his power,
The famine all his fulness brings ;
The plague presents his healing wings,
  And nature's final hour.

Whatever ills the world befall
A pledge of endless good we call,
  A sign of Jesus near ;
His chariot will not long delay ;
We hear the rumbling wheels, and pray—
  Triumphant Lord, appear !

LANGHORN'S "IT IS TOLD ME I MUST DIE."

FRAGMENTS of a somewhat remarkable poem have
been for a long period floating about in literature, and
inquiries have frequently been made in regard to their
authorship and origin. One of these fragments is entitled, " It is told me I must die."

In order to understand the poem, it will be necessary to review a somewhat tragic chapter of English history, known as the Popish Plot.

This popular madness was incited partly by the intrigues of Rome, and a remembrance of papal persecutions in the past, and partly by one of the most corrupt and infamous men on record, Titus Oates. He was born in 1620, was educated at Cambridge, took orders, but soon lost his curacies by lying, perjury, and gross misbehavior. He received an appointment as chaplain in the navy, but was dismissed for disgraceful conduct. He then became a Catholic, went to Spain, but was shortly expelled by the Jesuits.

In September, 1667, he made a disclosure before Sir Edward Godfrey, a noted justice, and afterwards before the Council and the House of Commons, to the effect that the Catholics had entered into a conspiracy against the life of the king, in order to reëstablish the papal power in England. Lord Arundel, he said, was to be chancellor of the new government; Lord Powis, treasurer; Lord Bellasis, general of the papal army, and Coleman, secretary of state. The office of advocate-general he assigned to Richard Langhorn, the subject of this paper.

All England was thrown into a state of intense excitement by this disclosure, and the fame of Titus Oates flashed forth to blaze "the comet of a season." "The capital and the whole nation," says Macaulay, "went mad with hatred and fear. London had the aspect of a city in a state of siege. Patrols marched up and down the streets. Cannon were planted around Whitehall.

No citizen thought himself safe unless he carried under his coat a small flail, loaded with lead, to brain the assassins." Oates rose from beggary to sudden wealth, and assumed a grandeur of living becoming a prince. He went around with a retinue of guards. He received an ample pension, and was assigned lodgings at Whitehall. He put on the Episcopal gown and cassock, and claimed and received the title of the "Saviour of the Nation." "Whoever he pointed at," says Roger North, "was taken up and committed." He had the nation in his hands, and for weeks of popular blindness, excitement and prejudice, he exercised an even greater influence than the king. He was the real sovereign of the English nation.

The state trials growing out of the so-called Popish Plot, are among the most interesting in history. Among these, with the exception of that of Lord Stafford, none are more interesting than that of Richard Langhorn. It took place on the 14th of June, 1679, and, although the testimony of Oates was again and again proven false, Langhorn's case was prejudged; he was convicted of high treason, and sentenced to be executed.

Langhorn, though by birth and education a Catholic, was a man of moderate views and deep spiritual feelings. Few men were ever more unjustly accused or more hastily condemned.

It was midsummer, a calm July day, and a great concourse of people came together to see Richard Langhorn hung. He ascended the scaffold as one would go to a coronation. With a bearing which told that every word he uttered was true, he said, "I do declare, in the presence of the eternal God, and as I hope to be saved by the merits of my dear Jesus, that I am not guilty, directly or indirectly, of any crime that has been sworn against me." He declared further that the testimony of Mr. Oates against him was wholly false, and that he forgave him with his dying breath, and hoped that God would bring him to repentance. He prayed for the king, the nation, and for all his enemies and false accusers. He forgave the sheriff after the rope had been adjusted. His last prayer and last words were, "Blessed Jesus, into thy hands I recommend my soul and spirit, now, at this instant. Take me into paradise." He added, "I am desirous to be with my Jesus. I am ready, and you need stop no longer for me."

Langhorn desired to be left entirely by himself in his last days, that he might give his time to meditation, writing, and acts of devotion. These days were passed on the heavenly border. The glory of the celestial world seemed already shining about him. His soul was immersed in the love of God.

It was thus in the solitude of his cell that he composed the irregular poem to which we have alluded. It is a most triumphant witness to the all-conquering power of the Christian faith. It is as follows:

IT IS TOLD ME I MUST DIE.

IT is told me I must die.
Oh, happy news !
Come on, my dearest soul,
Behold thy Jesus calls thee.
He prayed for thee upon his cross,

There he extended his arms to receive thee,
There he bowed down his head to kiss thee,
There he cried out with a powerful voice,
    " Father, receive him, he is mine !"
There he opened his heart to give thee entrance,
There he gave up his life to purchase life for thee!

It is told me I must die.
    Oh blessed news !
I must quit
    Earth for heaven,
    My earthly prison for a liberty of joy;
    My banishment for my country
        Prepared for me.
I must pass
    From time to eternity;
    From misery to felicity;
    From change to immutability;
    From death to immortality.
I must leave what I possess on earth,
    To possess my God;
      To enjoy my Jesus;
    To converse with angels and saints.
I must go to fill
    My spirit with a plenitude of light;
    My will with a fulness of peace;
    My memory with a collection of all good;
    My senses with a satiety of pleasures.
I must go where I shall find
    All things which I can desire,
    Nothing that I fear.
I shall no more want any good;
    God shall be unto me all in all,
    And my all to all eternity.

      It is told me I must die.
        Oh what happiness !

I am going

To the place of my rest;
To the land of the living;
To the haven of security;
To the kingdom of peace;
To the palace of my God;
To the nuptials of the Lamb;
To sit at the table of my King;
To feed on the bread of angels;
To see what no eye hath seen;
To hear what no ear hath heard;
To enjoy what the heart of man cannot comprehend.

It is told me I must die.

Oh news of joy!

Let us go, my soul, I am content;
  I joyfully renounce this life,
And render it back to Him who gave it me.
  I am willing to die

For his glory,

For his love,

Out of gratitude for his favors,

And to satisfy his justice.

I am willing to die for him as he died for me:
  · I am willing to die,

To see my Jesus,

To love my Jesus,

To bless my Jesus,

And to sing his praises to all eternity.
Come on, my soul, let us go and rejoice.

He who by his grace

Hath enabled thee to know

Thy own miseries,

And his mercies,

He who hath enabled thee

To rely on him,

Commands thee to shake off all fear.

It is not for anything in thee
That he loves thee and will save thee.
He doth it because he is God,
Perfect love and perfect goodness.
Oh my Father,
Oh thou best of all fathers,
Have pity on the most wretched of all thy children.
I was lost, but by thy mercy found;
I was dead, but by thy mercy raised again.
I was gone astray after vanity,
But am now ready to appear before thee.

Oh my Father,
Come now in mercy receive thy child:
Give him thy kiss of peace;
Remit unto him all his sins;
Clothe him with thy nuptial robe;
Receive him into thy house;
Permit him to have a place at thy feast,
And forgive all those who are guilty of his death.

The name of Langhorn well deserves a place among those worthies who, although associated by the influences of birth, education, and the force of circumstances with a corrupt church, have so fully relied on Christ as to keep their spiritual perceptions undimmed. " Thou hast a few names even in Sardis, which have not defiled their garments: and they shall walk with me in white; for they are worthy."

III. SONGS IN THE PILGRIMAGE.

1. *LORD, DISMISS US WITH THY BLESSING.*
2. *PEACE, TROUBLED SOUL*
3. *SWEET THE MOMENTS RICH IN BLESSING.*
4. *WATCHMAN, TELL US OF THE NIGHT.*
5. *WHILE THEE I SEEK, PROTECTING POWER.*
6. *HARK, THE VOICE OF LOVE AND MERCY.*
7. *WHEN MARSHALLED ON THE NIGHTLY PLAIN.*
8. *WHILE WITH CEASELESS COURSE THE SUN.*
9. *ON THE MOUNTAIN-TOP APPEARING.*
10. *IF I MUST DIE, OH, LET ME DIE TRUSTING IN JESUS' BLOOD.*
11. *AWAKE MY SOUL, IN JOYFUL LAYS.*

SONGS IN THE PILGRIMAGE.

"SWEET THE MOMENTS, RICH IN BLESSING."

THE personal history of few writers of popular hymns is so little known at the present time, as that of Sir Walter Shirley, author of "Sweet the moments, rich in blessing," "Peace, troubled soul, whose plaintive moan," and "Lord, dismiss us with thy blessing." And yet the lives of few hymn-writers abound with more impressive and highly interesting incidents. Shirley wrote but few hymns, but these have a popularity commensurate with their merits, and seem likely to prove enduring. With the single exception of Bishop Ken's "Doxology," and Perronet's "All hail the power of Jesus' name," no hymn is more universally used in public service than the following :

> LORD, dismiss us with thy blessing,
>   Fill our hearts with joy and peace ;
> Let us each, thy love possessing,
>   Triumph in redeeming grace :
>   Oh refresh us,
>   Travelling through this wilderness.
>
> Thanks we give, and adoration,
>   For thy gospel's joyful sound ;
> May the fruits of thy salvation
>   In our hearts and lives abound ;
>   May thy presence
>   With us evermore be found.

> Then, whene'er the signal's given
> Us from earth to call away,
> Borne on angels' wings to heaven—
> Glad the summons to obey—
> May we ever
> Reign with Christ in endless day.

The Hon. and Rev. Walter Shirley was born in the year 1725. He was brother to Earl Ferrars, and first cousin of Selina, Countess of Huntingdon. He was a frequent visitor to Lady Huntingdon's London residence, and there became acquainted with the Calvinist Methodist preachers. He was converted under the ministry of Mr. Venn, became intimate with Whitefield, took orders, and began to preach in the Church of England. After preaching with great success in his native country, he received the living of Loughrea, Ireland, where he continued to exercise his ministry for many years.

In the year 1760 he was called to endure severe discipline, which had the effect of making him deeply humble. While Sir Walter had been receiving the truths of the gospel, and growing in Christian graces, his brother, Earl Ferrars, had been leading a most worldly and licentious life, which, after years of secret dishonor, ended in public shame. In the year mentioned he became greatly incensed with a Mr. Johnson, his steward, who had been a servant in the family for thirty years, and who had shown a good disposition towards Lady Ferrars in her case against a favorite mistress of the nobleman. The details of the whole case are too unprofitable for recital; but the earl finding his old servant fearlessly devoted to his duty, deliberately shot him, and made no concealment of the deed. The murder proved a shock to English society. The earl was arrested and lodged in the Tower of London. He was brought to trial in Westminster, on which occasion, according to Charles Wesley, "most of the royal family, the chief gentry, and foreign ministers were present." After three days' sitting, the court sentenced the earl to be hanged at Tyburn, and "his body to be delivered to Surgeons' Hall to be dissected and anatomized."

The distress of Walter Shirley, Lady Huntingdon, and other pious relatives of the doomed earl, was extreme. The whole English church, and especially the then portion of it known as the Methodists, deeply sympathized with Walter Shirley. The conduct of the high-born convict now gave a still darker aspect and more heartrending associations to the crime. He resolved to die as hardened as he had lived.

Walter Shirley left his humble parish in Ireland and hastened to England, and, with Lady Huntingdon, did everything in his power to bring his brother to repentance and the exercise of religious faith, but without success. The religious society of London was deeply affected; prayers were offered up for the earl in the churches, and the Methodist societies spent a day in fasting and prayer for the unhappy nobleman's conversion. But all was of no avail. He spent the night before his execution in playing piquet with the warden of the prison. Just before leaving his cell on the fatal day, he wrote the following lines, which he left on the table:

11*

> " In doubt I lived, in doubt I die,
>   Yet stand prepared the vast abyss to try,
>   And undismayed expect eternity."

He went to Tyburn amid the tears of his friends and the derision of immense crowds of people. He dressed himself for execution in his wedding clothes, and received a note in his carriage from the wretched woman who had occasioned all this misery.

Sir Walter returned to his little flock in Loughrea a broken-spirited man. Three weeks after the execution he wrote to Mr. John Wesley as follows: "I have reason to bless God for the humbling lessons he has taught me through these awful visitations." It is probable that family misfortune was the source of the inspiration of his well-known hymn :

> PEACE, troubled soul, whose plaintive moan
>   Hath taught these rocks the notes of woe;
> Cease thy complaint—suppress thy groan,
>   And let thy tears forget to flow;
> Behold the precious balm is found,
> To lull thy pain, to heal thy wound.
>
> Come, freely come, by sin oppressed,
>   Unburden here thy weighty load;
> Here find thy refuge and thy rest,
>   And trust the mercy of thy God:
> Thy God's thy Saviour—glorious word!
> For ever love and praise the Lord.

Shirley opposed Wesley in forming societies outside of the Established Church. "I have hitherto learned to consider the Methodists," he wrote to Mr. Wesley, "not as any sect, but as a purer part of the Church of England." In the great religious controversy between the Arminian and Calvinist Methodists, Shirley sympathized with the views of Whitefield and Lady Huntingdon.

He greatly loved his little parish in Ireland, and was influenced with warm zeal for the conversion of souls. His piety and humility grew with advancing years, and he fully felt the power of the experience which he has so delightfully sung:

> SWEET the moments, rich in blessing,
>   Which before the cross I spend,
> Life, and health, and peace possessing
>   From the sinner's dying Friend.
>
> Here I rest, for ever viewing
>   Mercy poured in streams of blood;
> Precious drops, my soul bedewing,
>   Plead and claim my peace with God.
>
> Truly blessed is the station,
>   Low before his cross to lie,
> While I see divine compassion
>   Beaming in his languid eye.
>
> Lord, in ceaseless contemplation
>   Fix my thankful heart on thee,
> Till I taste thy full salvation,
>   And thine unveiled glory see.

This beautiful hymn is said to have been suggested by a religious poem written by James Allen, a local poet, which begins, " While my Jesus I 'm possessing."

His last days were serene and peaceful, and he witnessed to the end the power of Christian consolations. His sickness was protracted. When no longer able to leave the house, he was unwilling to cease preaching. The old man used to send for his neighbors, and, sitting in his chair in his own house, used to preach to as many as could hear him. He died in 1786.

His hymns are marked " Episcopal Collection " in some of the most widely used hymn-books. In several denominational, collections of hymns, his hymn beginning, " Lord, dismiss us with thy blessing," is attributed to Burder. It appeared originally in Harris' collection of hymns. The last lines of the second verse in the original are,

> " Ever faithful
> To thy truth may we be found."

" WATCHMAN, TELL US OF THE NIGHT."

> WATCHMAN, tell us of the night,
>   What its signs of promise are.
> Trav'ler, o'er yon mountain's height
>   See the glory-beaming star.
> Watchman, does its beauteous ray
>   Aught of hope or joy foretell?
> Trav'ler, yes, it brings the day—
>   Promised day of Israel.
>
> Watchman, tell us of the night;
>   Higher yet that star ascends.
> Trav'ler, blessedness and light,
>   Peace and truth, its course portends.
> Watchman, will its beams, alone,
>   Gild the spot that gave them birth?
> Trav'ler, ages are its own;
>   See, it bursts o'er all the earth.

> Watchman, tell us of the night,
>   For the morning seems to dawn.
> Trav'ler, darkness takes its flight;
>   Doubt and terror are withdrawn.
> Watchman, let thy wandering cease:
>   Hie thee to thy quiet home.
> Trav'ler, lo! the Prince of Peace,
>   Lo! the Son of God is come.

This hymn was written by Sir John Bowring in 1825. Mr. Bowring seems to have been an almost prophetic poet, and, like Isaiah, to have had continually in view the spiritual victories that are to fill the world with righteousness. In every high position he took with him a hopeful, luminous Christian experience, and ever seemed like a watchman on the walls of Zion, who sooner than others saw and heralded the first beams of the full-orbed and glorious gospel day.

He was born in Exeter in 1792. He was a precocious youth, and possessed a remarkable power in acquiring the languages. He became highly accomplished, was elected to Parliament, was appointed consul at Canton, made governor of Hong Kong, and received the honor of knighthood. His Christian experience, and his hopes and expectations of the spread of the gospel over the whole world, are beautifully portrayed in his "Matins and Vespers."

"WHILE THEE I SEEK, PROTECTING POWER."

> While thee I seek, protecting Power,
>   Be my vain wishes stilled;
> And may this consecrated hour
>   With better hopes be filled.

Thy love the power of thought bestowed;
  To thee my thoughts would soar:
Thy mercy o'er my life has flowed;
  That mercy I adore.

In each event of life, how clear
  Thy ruling hand I see;
Each blessing to my soul most dear,
  Because conferred by thee.

In every joy that crowns my days,
  In every pain I bear,
My heart shall find delight in praise,
  Or seek relief in prayer.

When gladness wings my favored hour
  Thy love my thoughts shall fill;
Resigned when storms of sorrow lower,
  My soul shall meet thy will.

My lifted eye, without a tear,
  The gathering storm shall see:
My steadfast heart shall know no fear;
  That heart will rest on thee.

Some expressions of this hymn have indirect reference to the stormy scenes in France about the time of the Revolution. It was written in France when the political sky was very dark and threatening, and no one felt secure. Its author was Miss Helen Maria Williams. She was born in the North of England in 1762. She went to London at the age of eighteen, where she won much reputation as a poet. She afterwards went to Paris, where she lived during the breaking up of the monarchy, and where she published works in prose and verse. She was a very devout woman, and relied on the strong arm of God at the time of peril.   She held a high place in religious society, both in London and Paris.

———•———

"*HARK! THE VOICE OF LOVE AND MERCY.*"

HARK! the voice of love and mercy
  Sounds aloud from Calvary;
See! it rends the rocks asunder,
  Shakes the earth, and veils the sky;
    "It is finished!"
  Hear the dying Saviour cry.

It is finished! Oh what pleasure
  Do these charming words afford!
Heavenly blessings without measure
  Flow to us from Christ the Lord:
    It is finished:
  Saints, the dying words record.

Tune your harps anew, ye seraphs
  Join to sing the pleasing theme;
All on earth and all in heaven
  Join to praise Immanuel's name;
    It is finished:
  Glory to the bleeding Lamb.

This hymn is the fruit of a remarkable Christian experience; a grateful expression of a sense of the greatness of God's mercy, and the extent of the atonement which the writer had occasion to feel.   It was written by Jonathan Evans about the year 1787, and appeared in "Rippon's Selection," under the title of "Finished Redemption."

Mr. Evans was in early life a very irreligious man. He was employed in a ribbon factory, and led a very profitless and unpromising life, until he was nearly thirty years of age, when he became converted, and joined the Congregationalists.   Soon after his conversion he began to speak of God's dealings with him, in public, preaching at such times as his secular employments permitted. He at last gathered around him a church and began a stated ministry.

"*WHEN, MARSHALLED ON THE NIGHTLY PLAIN.*"

HENRY KIRKE WHITE was born at Nottingham, England, 1785.   His father was a butcher in very humble circumstances.   At the age of fourteen he became a weaver's apprentice, and two years later he was articled to an attorney.

His religious experience is interesting.   He had an intimate friend in youth, named Almond.   White was a skeptic, and used to ridicule religion and religious things ; while Almond's heart was open to conviction ; he seemed anxious to know the truth and to practise it.

One day Almond was called to the bedside of a dying believer, who passed away in great peace, consoled by a triumphant faith.   He was fully convinced of the truth of religion by the impressive scene, and resolved to become a Christian.   But he shrunk from making known his convictions through fear of the ridicule of White.

His mind for a time was greatly agitated and divided, but he at last made the resolution to give up the society of his friend, should it be necessary, and to avow himself a believer in Christ.

White felt the neglect of his friend keenly, and went to him in an injured way, and inquired the cause. Almond confessed the change that had taken place in his views, and announced his purpose of leading a different life. The answer, of course, implied that his friend was unworthy the confidence of one who aimed to live piously. White saw it in this light, and was cut to the quick.

"Good God, Almond!" exclaimed the conscience-smitten skeptic, "you surely regard me in a worse light than I deserve."

The interview melted the heart of White, and he, too, became an inquirer after truth, embraced religion, and the two youths renewed their friendship with warmer feelings and more elevated aims.

This experience White relates metaphorically in his familiar hymn which follows:

> WHEN, marshalled on the nightly plain,
>   The glittering host bestud the sky,
> One star alone of all the train
>   Can fix the sinner's wandering eye.
> Hark, hark! to God the chorus breaks,
>   From every host, from every gem;
> But one alone the Saviour speaks;
>   It is the Star of Bethlehem.
>
> Once on the raging seas I rode:
>   The storm was loud, the night was dark;
> The ocean yawned, and rudely blowed
>   The wind that tossed my foundering bark.
> Deep horror then my vitals froze,
>   Death-struck, I ceased the tide to stem,
> When suddenly a star arose,
>   It was the Star of Bethlehem.

It was my guide, my light, my all,
  It bade my dark forebodings cease;
And through the storm and danger's thrall,
  It led me to the port of peace.
Now, safely moored, my perils o'er,
  I 'll sing, first in night's diadem,
For ever and for evermore,
  The Star, the Star of Bethlehem !

White now turned his purpose of life to the ministry, and prepared himself for Cambridge by severe study. At college his health gave way under the severity of his application, and he died in the autumn of 1806, at the age of twenty.

"WHILE WITH CEASELESS COURSE THE SUN."

WHILE with ceaseless course the sun
  Hasted through the former year,
Many souls their race have run,
  Never more to meet us here:
Fixed in an eternal state,
  They have done with all below;
We a little longer wait,
  But how little—none can know.

As the wingéd arrow flies
  Speedily the mark to find,
As the lightning from the skies
  Darts and leaves no trace behind,
Swiftly thus our fleeting days
  Bear us down life's rapid stream;
Upward, Lord, our spirits raise:
  All below is but a dream.

Thanks for mercies past receive,
　Pardon of our sins renew;
Teach us henceforth how to live
　With eternity in view.
Bless thy word to young and old;
　Fill us with a Saviour's love;
And, when life's short tale is told,
　May we dwell with thee above.

This hymn was written by the Rev. John Newton, for the " Olney Hymns." Mr. Newton calls his hymns " The fruit and expression of his own experience." The allusion in the first stanza of the hymn has reference to the changes that had taken place in his own parish at Olney, where he was, at the time of the writing, a very active and sympathizing curate.

* * *

"ON THE MOUNTAIN-TOP APPEARING."

THOMAS KELLY, an admired hymn-writer and an excellent and useful clergyman, was the son of the Hon. Chief Baron Kelly of Dublin, and was born in 1769. He was educated in Dublin University, and was partly prepared to enter the profession of law, when he became deeply impressed with the instability of worldly things and the magnitude of spiritual riches, and decided to enter the ministry. He was ordained in the Established Church at the age of twenty-four. He began to labor with great zeal for the conversion of souls, preaching the doctrine of justification by faith. This course was deemed by his friends a departure from the dignity of of his office, and was deeply humiliating to his high-born family, who for a time treated him with marked coolness and disregard. "To go to the stake," he said, "would be a less trial to me than to so set myself against those whom I so dearly love." But he remained firm to his convictions of duty, and multitudes flocked to his preaching, and he was able to exert a very powerful influence. He was an Oriental scholar and a musical composer, as well as a poet, but he laid all of his varied gifts and accomplishments, with unaffected simplicity and humility, at the foot of the Cross.

His religious experience is related in the following hymn :

> Poor and afflicted, Lord, are thine,
> Among the great they seldom shine;
> Yet though the world may think it strange,
> They would not with the world exchange.
>
> Poor and afflicted—'t is their lot;
> They know it, and they murmur not;
> 'T would ill become them to refuse
> The state their Maker deigned to choose.
>
> Poor and afflicted—yet they sing;
> For Jesus is their glorious King;
> Through sufferings perfect now he reigns,
> And shares in all their griefs and pains.
>
> And while they walk the thorny way
> They 're often heard to sigh and say
> Dear Saviour come, oh, quickly come,
> And take thy mourning pilgrims home.

The lines, as applied to his own case, are not in the strictest sense true, for he was a man of large wealth. He wrote more than seven hundred hymns of many degrees of excellence. He was dissatisfied with the discipline of the Established Church; entertained broad views, and looked for the coming of Christ's universal kingdom. This experience is the origin of his well-known hymn:

On the mountain-top appearing,
  Lo the sacred herald stands,
Joyful news to Zion bearing,
  Zion long in hostile hands:
    Mourning captive,
  God himself shall loose thy bands.

Has thy night been long and mournful?
  Have thy friends unfaithful proved?
Have thy foes been proud and scornful,
  By thy sighs and tears unmoved?
    Cease thy mourning;
  Zion still is well beloved.

God, thy God, will now restore thee;
  He himself appears thy Friend;
All thy foes shall flee before thee;
  Here their boasts and triumphs end
    Great deliverance
  Zion's King will surely send.

Peace and joy shall now attend thee;
  All thy warfare now is past;
God thy Saviour will defend thee;
  Victory is thine at last:
    All thy conflicts
  End in everlasting rest.

He labored in Dublin for more than sixty years. Lord Plunkett, one of his intimate friends, once said to him,

"I think you will live to a great age."

"I am confident I shall," said the vicar; "I expect never to die."

His dying testimony was to this effect: "The Lord is my all in all."

"IF I MUST DIE, OH LET ME DIE TRUSTING IN JESUS' BLOOD."

BENJAMIN BEDDOME, a Baptist minister, lived a life of comparative seclusion in a small country village, called Bourton-on-the-Water, Gloucestershire, where he died September, 1795, in the 79th year of his age. He was a religious poet, and wrote nearly one thousand hymns.

In 1749 he was prostrated by a very severe illness, and on his recovery wrote a hymn, which, after some improving, was published as follows:

> IF I must die, oh let me die
>   Trusting in Jesus' blood,
> That blood which full atonement made
>   And reconciles to God.
>
> If I must die, then let me die
>   In peace with all mankind,
> And change these fleeting joys below
>   For pleasures all refined.
>
> If I must die, as die I must,
>   Let some kind seraph come,
> And bear me on his friendly wing
>   To my celestial home.

Of Canaan's land, from Pisgah's top,
  May I but have a view,
Though Jordan should o'erflow its banks,
  I 'll boldly venture through.

His death fulfilled the expectations of the hymn. He preached long after the silver crown of age had been set upon his head, and venerableness had added solemnity and dignity to his words. He desired that he might depart without a long sickness. He was confined to his house at last only a single Lord's day. An hour before his death he was found composing a hymn, in which was the following stanza:

"God of my life and of my choice,
  Shall I no longer hear thy voice?
Oh let the source of joy divine
  With rapture fill this heart of mine."

————♦————

"AWAKE, MY SOUL, IN JOYFUL LAYS."

Rev. Samuel Medley was born in Hertfordshire, England, 1738. At the age of eighteen he entered the navy, and was wounded in the engagement off Cape Lagos, under Admiral Boscawen, in 1759. His wound proved a very serious one.

"I am afraid," said the surgeon, "that amputation is the only thing that will save your life. I can tell to-morrow morning."

Medley had received religious instruction from a pious father and grandfather, and had been made the subject of frequent prayer. He had led a profligate life in the navy, but the pious lessons of his early youth returned upon him at the surgeon's awful warning, and he remembered that God was a Helper when human helps fail. He began to pray, and passed a part of the night in prayer. The next morning the surgeon came to examine his wounds, and lifted his hands in surprise at the favorable change that had taken place. "This," said he, "is little short of a miracle."

Medley now resolved to lead a religious life, but on recovery was again led into thoughtless habits.

Returning to his home, he was compelled to listen to many a faithful admonition and warning. One Sabbath evening he inquired of a servant if his grandfather was going out to worship. "No," was the answer, "he is coming to read a sermon to you." "A sermon to me!" replied Medley; "he had better be anywhere else!" The sermon was one by Dr. Watts, from Isaiah 42:6, 7. He listened to it at first with indifference, but his heart at last began to melt, and he was led to see the wonderful forbearance of God. As soon as the aged man left him alone, he fell upon his knees, and not long after the love of Christ filled his soul and changed the purpose of his life. His best known hymn is a relation of this experience:

> AWAKE, my soul, in joyful lays,
> And sing thy great Redeemer's praise;
> He justly claims a song from me;
> His loving-kindness is so free!
>
> He saw me ruined in the fall,
> Yet loved me notwithstanding all:
> He saved me from my lost estate;
> His loving-kindness is so great!

Through mighty hosts of cruel foes,
Where earth and hell my way oppose,
He safely leads my soul along!
His loving-kindness is so strong!

When earthly friends forsake me quite,
And I have neither skill nor might,
He's sure my helper to appear;
His loving-kindness is so near!

Often I feel my sinful heart
Prone from my Jesus to depart;
And though I oft have him forgot,
His loving-kindness changes not.

So when I pass death's gloomy vale,
And life and mortal powers shall fail,
Oh may my last expiring breath
His loving-kindness sing in death!

IV. SUNDAY-SCHOOL HYMNS.

1. *SHEPHERD OF TENDER YOUTH.*
2. *THERE IS A HAPPY LAND.*
3. *I THINK WHEN I READ THAT SWEET STORY OF OLD.*
4. *WE SPEAK OF THE REALMS OF THE BLEST.*
5. *NOW I LAY ME DOWN TO SLEEP.*
6. *GOLDEN HEAD, SO LOWLY BENDING.*
7. *"NOW I LAY,"—REPEAT IT, DARLING.*
8. *I WANT TO BE AN ANGEL.*
9. *'TIS RELIGION THAT CAN GIVE.*
10. *STAND UP FOR JESUS.*
11. *DAILY, DAILY SING THE PRAISES.*
12. *JUST AS I AM, WITHOUT ONE PLEA.*
13. *BY COOL SILOAM'S SHADY RILL.*
14. *O MOTHER DEAR, JERUSALEM.*
15. *JERUSALEM, MY HAPPY HOME.*
16. *I'M BUT A STRANGER HERE*
17. *GOD CALLING YET.*
18. *LITTLE TRAVELLERS ZIONWARD.*
19. *LAND AHEAD! ITS FRUITS ARE WAVING.*
20. *HE LEADETH ME! OH, BLESSED THOUGHT.*
21. *I AM SO GLAD THAT OUR FATHER IN HEAVEN*
22. *I GAVE MY LIFE FOR THEE.*

SUNDAY-SCHOOL HYMNS.

THE writers of the best Sunday-school hymns are benefactors, whose influence is hardly calculable, but whose personal history, with but few exceptions, is little known.

1. The following is a part of the oldest Christian hymn for children :

SHEPHERD of tender youth,
Guiding in love and truth
  Through devious ways,
Christ, our triumphant king,
We come thy name to sing,
And here our children bring
  To shout thy praise.

Ever be thou our guide,
Our shepherd and our pride,
  Our staff and song;
Jesus, thou Christ of God,
By thy perennial word
Lead us where thou hast trod,
  Make our faith strong.

So now, and till we die
Sound we thy praises high,
  And joyful sing;
Infants, and the glad throng
Who to thy church belong,
Unite and sing the song
  To Christ our king.

2. The favorite Sunday-school hymn beginning —

" There is a happy land,"

seems to have been suggested by a Hebrew melody.   It
was written by Andrew Young, a cultured Scotchman,
and a popular teacher of youth.   In 1830, he was elected
by the City Council of Edinburgh, head master of the
Niddry street school, and in 1840 was appointed English
master in Madras college.   He held the latter position
thirteen years, and has since resided in Edinburgh.

3. The hymn beginning—

" I think when I read that sweet story of old,"

which is sometimes attributed to Mrs. Judson, was composed by Mrs. Jemima Luke, a benevolent and accomplished English lady, born at Colebrook Terrace, Islington,
August 19, 1813.   She took a great interest in missionary enterprises, and for several years edited *The Missionary Repository.* She exhibited a fine literary and poetic
taste early in life, and at the age of thirteen was able to
write acceptably for the *Juvenile Magazine.*   The hymn
was composed under somewhat peculiar circumstances,
and she had no idea of its value or ultimate popularity
at the time of writing.   Her father, Thomas Thompson,
Esq., was a philanthropist, and took an interest, like herself, in missions, and in the education of poor children.
Mrs. Luke became much attached to a little village
school near her father's residence at Pondsford Park,
and, on a certain occasion, wished to write a little song
for it, that would awaken an interest in religion and
have a salutary effect on the minds of the children.   The

leading thought of the hymn, which is Christ's present sympathy for the little ones, was brought to her mind while riding in a stage-coach, and she composed the poem during the ride, while the inspiration of the subject yet lingered.   It was published in 1865.

The following is the original of Mrs. Luke's beautiful hymn, which has two stanzas not found in many collections :

> I THINK when I read that sweet story of old,
> When Jesus dwelt here among men,
> How he called little children as lambs to his fold,
> I should like to have been with him then.
>
> I wish that his hand had been put on my head,
> And that I been placed on his knee,
> And that I might have seen his kind look when he said,
> " Let the little ones come unto me."
>
> Yet still to his footstool in prayer I may go,
> And ask for a share in his love ;
> And if I thus earnestly seek him below,
> I shall hear him and see him above,
>
> In that beautiful place he is gone to prepare
> For all who are washed and forgiven ;
> And many dear children are gathering there,
> For of such is the kingdom of heaven.
>
> But thousands and thousands who wander and fall
> Never heard of that heavenly home ;
> I should like them to know there is room for them all
> And that Jesus has bid them to come.
>
> I long for that blessed and glorious time—
> The fairest, the brightest, the best—
> When the dear little children of every clime
> Shall crowd to his arms and be blessed.

4. The hymn found in nearly all Sunday-school collections, entitled "What must it be to be there?" and beginning—

"We speak of the realms of the blest,"

was written by a young English lady, the wife of Thomas Mills, Esq., M. P., who was much esteemed for her amiableness, tenderness of feeling, and calm religious trust. She died at the age of twenty-four. The hymn was composed about three weeks before her decease, while she was yet lingering, as it were, on the heavenly border refreshed with the near prospect of Paradise. She had been reading Bridges on Psalm 119:44, "We speak of heaven, but, oh, to be there!" The original has six stanzas.

5. The little prayer beginning—

"Now I lay me down to sleep,"

is altered from Dr. Watts. It has been an evening prayer for children, as far as the English language is spoken, for nearly two centuries. Several little Sunday-school ballads have been written upon it.

6. One of these first appeared in *Putnam's Magazine:*

GOLDEN head, so lowly bending,
  Little feet so white and bare,
Dewy eyes, half shut, half opened,
  Lisping out her evening prayer.

Well she knows when she is saying
  "Now I lay me down to sleep,"
'T is to God that she is praying,
  Praying him her soul to keep.

Half asleep, and murmuring faintly
  "If I should die before I wake"—
Tiny fingers clasped so saintly—
  "I pray the Lord my soul to take."

Oh the rapture, sweet, unbroken,
  Of the soul who wrote that prayer!
Children's myriad voices floating
  Up to heaven record it there.

If, of all that has been written,
  I could choose what might be mine,
It should be that child's petition,
  Rising to the throne divine.

7. The following, entitled " The unfinished Prayer,"
originally appeared, we think, in the *Lutheran Home
Monthly:*

" Now I lay,"—repeat it, darling—
  "Lay me," lisped the tiny lips
Of my daughter, kneeling, bending
  O'er her folded finger tips.

" Down to sleep"—"To sleep," she murmured,
  And the curly head bent low;
" I pray the Lord"—I gently added,
  " You can say it all I know."

" Pray the Lord—" The sound came faintly,
  Fainter still—" My soul to keep;"
Then the tired head fairly nodded,
  And the child was fast asleep.

But the dewy eyes half opened
  When I clasped her to my breast,
And the dear voice softly whispered,
  " Mamma, God knows all the rest.

13*

8. Rev. Dr. Armitage of New York, in a lecture on "Our Female Hymn Writers," has recently brought to light the touching history of the hymn, beginning,

> "I want to be an angel."

"It was written," he says, "by Mrs. Sydney P. Gill, in Philadelphia. In the Sunday-school of Dr. Joel Parker's church she taught the infant class. She had been teaching a lesson on angels, when a little child said, 'I want to be an angel.' A few days after, the child died, the hymn was written for that Sunday-school to sing on her death, and it has struck a chord in every child's heart since 1845."

It was composed April 19, 1845, on the day of the death of a little girl named Annie Louisa Farrand, the Sunday-school scholar to whom Dr. Armitage refers.

The words "I want to be an angel" had at this time been made familiar by the following incident, written by Dr. Irenæus Prime, April 5, 1845, which was being copied by nearly all religious and Sunday-school papers:

"A child sat in the door of a cottage at the close of a summer Sabbath. The twilight was fading, and as the shades of evening darkened, one after another of the stars stood in the sky and looked down on the child in his thoughtful mood. He was looking up at the stars and counting them as they came, till there were too many to be counted, and his eyes wandered all over the heavens, watching the bright worlds above. They seemed just like "holes in the floor of heaven to let the glory through," but he knew better. Yet he loved to look up there, and was so absorbed, that his mother called to him and said :

" ' My son, what are you thinking of ?'

" He started as if suddenly aroused from sleep, and answered,

" ' I was thinking———

" ' Yes,' said his mother, ' I know you were thinking, but what were you thinking about ?'

" ' Oh,' said he, and his little eyes sparkled with the thought, ' *I want to be an angel.*'

" ' And why, my son, would you be an angel ?'

" ' Heaven is up there, is it not, mother ? and there the angels live and love God, and are happy. I do wish I was good, and God would take me there, and let me wait on him for ever.'

" The mother called him to her knee, and he leaned on her bosom and wept. She wept too, and smoothed the soft hair of his head as he stood there, and kissed his forehead, and then told him that if he would give his heart to God, now while he was young, the Saviour would forgive all his sins and take him up to heaven when he died, and he would then be with God for ever.

"His young heart was comforted. He knelt at his mother's side and said :

> " ' Jesus, Saviour, Son of God,
> Wash me in thy precious blood ;
> I thy little lamb would be,
> Help me, Lord, to look to thee.

The mother took the young child to his chamber and soon he was asleep, dreaming perhaps of angels and heaven. A few months afterwards sickness was on him, and the light of that cottage, the joy of that mother's heart, went out. He breathed his last in her arms, and as he took her parting kiss, he whispered in her ear :

"'I am going to be an angel.'"

> 9. 'T is religion that can give
> Sweetest pleasure while we live ;
> 'T is religion can supply
> Solid comfort when we die.
> After death its joys shall be
> Lasting as eternity.

This poem, in six lines, is from an English book, by Mary Masters. In the preface to the work, we read, " The author of the following poems never read a treatise of rhetoric or an art of poetry, nor was ever taught her English grammar. Her education rose no higher than the spelling-book or her writing-master. Her genius to poetry was always discountenanced by her parents, and till her merit got the better of her fortune, she was shut out from all commerce with the more knowing and polite part of the world."

10. The American Sunday-school hymn, beginning,

"Stand up, stand up for Jesus,"

was composed by George Duffield, a Presbyterian clergyman in Detroit. He was born at Carlisle, Penn., in 1818, and graduated at Yale College in 1837. He has written a number of hymns, of which, " Stand up for Jesus," owing perhaps to its associations, is best known. It was composed to be sung after a sermon delivered by the writer on the sudden death of Rev. Dudley A. Tyng, whose dying words to his Christian brothers were, " Stand up for Jesus."

Dudley Atkins Tyng was born on the 12th of January, 1825, in a quiet parsonage in Prince George Co., Va. His father, Dr. Stephen H. Tyng, removed to St. George's Church, Philadelphia, in which parish Dudley passed his boyhood. He was a precocious scholar. He was able to read the Latin authors at the age of seven, and he entered the University of Pennsylvania at the age of fourteen.

He became the subject of converting grace and experimental religion in 1841. His father relates the following touching incident in connection with his conversion : " Late one night, when all the family had retired to rest, and left me to my closing hour of solitude in my study, I heard the sound of feet descending the stairs. It was this dear boy, who had risen from his bed in sleepless sorrow. As he came into my room and pressed his arms around my neck, he said, " Dear father, I cannot sleep, I am so sinful. Father, will you pray for me ?"

In 1854, Mr. Tyng became rector of the church of the Epiphany, Philadelphia, and he entered with glowing zeal and love for souls into the revival work associated with the great religious awakening which, soon after his instalment, manifested itself at Philadelphia and in the principal cities of the United States. He was the favorite leader of the great union prayer-meetings held in Philadelphia, and it is said that he met more inquirers during the revival than any other pastor in the city.

In the spring following the great awakening, he met with a terrible accident that proved fatal in its results. " Dr. ———," said the young pastor to his physician, " my friend   _n me up; they say that I am dying; is that   ..on?" The doctor replied in the affirmative.   ..en, doctor, I have something to say to you. I have loved you much as a friend ; I long to love you as a brother in Jesus Christ. Let me entreat you now to come to Jesus."

He was asked if he had any message to his brethren in the ministry. He said, addressing his father,

" Father, stand up for Jesus. Tell them, let us all stand up for Jesus."

He became partially unconscious. He did not know any of the members of the family.

" Do you know Jesus ?" he was asked.

His answer was jubilant.

" I know Jesus. I have a steadfast trust in Jesus—a calm and steadfast trust."

" Are you happy ?"

" Perfectly ! perfectly."

He was buried amid the tears of more than ten thousand people.

11. The English Sunday-school hymn, so popular in Episcopal churches, beginning,

> " Daily, daily sing the praises
> Of the city God has made,"

was composed by Sabine Baring-Gould, and originally printed on a card for the use of St. John's Mission, Horbury Bridge, Yorkshire. The same year it appeared in the "Church Times." The chorus is vigorous, and the music is animating as the hymn:

> "Oh that I had wings of angels
>   Here to spread and heavenwa.
> I would seek the walls of Zion,
>   Far beyond the starry sky."

12. The authorship of the hymn, beginning,

> "Just as I am, without one plea,"

has recently been noticed in several religious papers. It was written by Charlotte Elliott of Torquay, Eng. She was born March 18, 1789, and died at Brighton, Sept. 22, 1871. The original hymn has a stanza often omitted:

> "Just as I am, of that free love
> The breadth, length, depth, and height to prove,
> Here for a season, then above,
>   O Lamb of God, I come."

13. The favorite Sunday-school hymn, beginning,

> "By cool Siloam's shady rill,"

was composed by Bishop Heber. He but gives in it his own experience. His early feet "trod the paths of peace," and his mind was early "upward drawn to God." He was a solitary student at Oxford, his gentle, devotional nature shrinking from the show and affectation of society. His fine poem, "Palestine," was written for a college exercise. Though so quiet, he became greatly beloved at Oxford, and when "Palestine" was first read by him in the theatre, at the annual college commencement, it was received with such an outburst of applause as probably never before greeted an Oxford student. His aged father and mother were present on the occasion. After the reading of the poem, young Heber was for a long time missing, and his mother, going to look for him, softly opened the door of his sleeping room. She found him on his knees breathing out his soul in gratitude and prayer.

14. The hymn, used both in the church and Sunday-school, beginning,

> "O mother dear, Jerusalem,"

was written in the Tower of London on the Thames, during the reign of Elizabeth. Its figures and contrasts are those of imprisonment. Such lines as

> "Oh happy harbor of God's saints,"
> "There envy bears no sway,"
> "Thy turrets and thy pinnacles,"
> "We that are here in banishment,"

have new meanings as we understand the associations amid which they were written. Some of the stanzas, usually omitted in hymn-books, are very beautiful.

Its author was Francis Baker. It is also inscribed to David Dickson, 1583–1662.

> O MOTHER dear, Jerusalem!
>   When shall I come to thee?
> When shall my sorrows have an end?
>   Thy joys when shall I see?
>
> Oh happy harbor of God's saints!
>   Oh sweet and pleasant soil!
> In thee no sorrow can be found,
>   Nor grief nor care nor toil.

In thee no sickness is at all,
  Nor hurt nor any sore;
There is no death nor ugly sight,
  But life for evermore.

No murky cloud o'ershadows thee,
  Nor gloom, nor darksome night;
But every soul shines as the sun;
  For God himself gives light.

Jerusalem! Jerusalem!
  Would God I were in thee!
Oh that my sorrows had an end,
  Thy joys that I might see.

Thy turrets and thy pinnacles
  With carbuncles do shine,
With jasper, pearl, and chrysolite,
  Surpassing pure and fine.

Thy houses are of ivory,
  Thy windows crystal clear,
Thy streets are laid with beaten gold;
  There angels do appear.

Thy walls are made of precious stone,
  Thy bulwarks diamond square,
Thy gates are made of orient pearl;
  O God, if I were there!

Oh my sweet home, Jerusalem!
  Thy joys when shall I see?
The King that sitteth on thy throne
  In his felicity?

Thy gardens and thy goodly walks
  Continually are green,
Where grow such sweet and pleasant flowers
  As nowhere else are seen.

14

Right through thy streets with pleasing sound,
   The living waters flow,
And on the banks, on either side
   The trees of life do grow.

Those trees each month yield ripened fruit;
   For evermore they spring,
And all the nations of the earth
   To thee their honors bring.

If heaven be thus glorious, Lord,
   Why should I stay from thence?
What folly's this, that I should dread
   To die and go from hence!

Reach down, O Lord, thine arm of grace,
   And cause me to ascend
Where congregations ne'er break up
   And Sabbaths never end.

O mother dear, Jerusalem!
   When shall I come to thee?
When shall my sorrows have an end?
   Thy joys when shall I see?

15. The stanzas which follow, constituting a well-known and popular hymn by themselves, seem to have been formed on the same model:

JERUSALEM, my happy home,
   Name ever dear to me,
When shall my labors have an end
   In joy and peace and thee?

When shall these eyes thy heaven-built walls
   And pearly gates behold?
Thy bulwarks, with salvation strong,
   And streets of shining gold?

There happier bowers than Eden's bloom,
  Nor sin nor sorrow know:
Blest seats! through rude and stormy scenes
  I onward press to you.

Why should I shrink from pain and woe,
  Or feel at death dismay?
I 've Canaan's goodly land in view
  And realms of endless day.

Apostles, martyrs, prophets, there
  Around my Saviour stand:
And soon my friends in Christ below
  Will join the glorious band.

Jerusalem, my happy home,
  My soul still pants for thee;
Then shall my labors have an end,
  When I thy joys shall see.

16. Every Sunday-school scholar is familiar with the beautiful hymn, beginning,

> "I 'm but a stranger here,
> Heaven is my home."

Older and more experienced minds may have marked so much of evident sincerity and so little of the spirit of authorship in the lines, as to wish to know who was the author, and under what peculiar discipline of life they were composed. The hymn was written by Thomas Rawson Taylor, the son of an English Congregationalist minister. He was born near Wakefield on the 9th of May, 1807. At the age of fifteen he became a merchant's clerk, and he was subsequently apprenticed as a printer. While thus employed he became interested in the concerns of his soul, experienced great spiritual consolations in seasons of prayer, and was impressed that it was his duty to give up his secular calling and prepare for the ministry. He entered Airesdale College, where he remained three years, living a life of most elevated and self-forgetful piety. He did not wait to complete his education before he commenced active service in the cause of his Master. He seemed to feel the force of the Divine command, "Work while the day lasts." While a student he used to go out to the towns and villages near the college preaching the Word, and appearing in his young zeal like a special messenger of celestial truth. In July, 1830, he was received as minister at Haward street chapel at Sheffield. Here his health began to decline; it became evident that he was marked for an early death, and that his bright prospects of worldly usefulness were destined to be disappointed. The change gradually continued. He struggled against it for several years, and at times seemed to check the sure hand of the destroyer. But all remedial efforts proved in vain, and he died March 7, 1835.

In his altered days he felt that he was a "stranger here" in the world of life and activity. But as one by one his worldly hopes perished, and the things of earth lost their power to charm, he realized with glowing anticipations that "Heaven was his home.

I 'M but a stranger here,
Heaven is my home;
Earth is a desert drear,
Heaven is my home.

Dangers and sorrows stand
Round me on every hand;
Heaven is my Fatherland—
  Heaven is my home.

What though the tempest rage,
  Heaven is my home;
Short is my pilgrimage,
  Heaven is my home.
And time's wild, wintry blast
Soon will be overpast;
I shall reach home at last—
  Heaven is my home.

Therefore I murmur not,
  Heaven is my home;
Whate'er my earthly lot,
  Heaven is my home.
And I shall surely stand
There at my Lord's right hand—
Heaven is my Fatherland—
  Heaven is my home.

There at my Saviour's side,
  Heaven is my home;
I shall be glorified,
  Heaven is my home.
There are the good and blest,
Those I loved most and best,
There, too, I soon shall rest—
  Heaven is my home.

Taylor died young, and he must have felt like Keats, that his name was "writ in water," or, like Kirke White,

"I shall sink
As sinks the traveller in the crowded streets
Of busy London."

14*

But his little hymn, written amid the dreariness of worldly disappointment, has accomplished a mission that makes him a benefactor, and by it he yet speaks, as no living voice can speak, to almost countless congregations in nearly every part of the world.

17. The beautiful hymn which has lately become a favorite in the Sunday-school, Young People's meetings, and Inquiry meetings, beginning, "God calling yet," was written by Gerhard Tersteegen. Thousands who sing this hymn, and who also love to sing another precious stanza from a hymn by the same author, beginning—

> " Is there a thing beneath the sun,
>   That strives with Thee my heart to share ?"

know but little of the personal history of the writer. Others who love to read—

> "Thou hidden love of God, whose height—"

have never heard of the great religious happiness and elevation of soul that its German author enjoyed.

Gerhard Tersteegen, the original author of the hymns to which we have alluded, and one of the most eminent religious poets of the Reformed German church in its early days, was born in 1697, in the town of Mors, in Westphalia. He was left an orphan in boyhood by the death of his father, and as his mother's means were limited, he was put to work as an apprentice when very young at Muhlheim on the Rhur. Here, when about fifteen years of age, he became deeply concerned for his soul, and experienced a deep and abiding spiritual work. He was riding one day to Duisburg in a deep forest alone, when he suddenly fell ill, being thrown into violent convulsions that threatened his life. He fell upon his knees and implored God to spare his life, that he might prepare for eternity. He experienced almost immediate relief, and at once dedicated his life to Christ. An inward conflict followed, for his early religious comforts seem to have been like wandering lights, now vanishing and now appearing. He used to express this state of his experience in the words of St. Augustine:

> "My heart is pained, nor can it be
> At rest, till it finds rest in Thee."

But his religious perceptions became clearer; the fountains of heavenly refreshment were opened; his soul entered into the rest of divine love, and found in it a present heaven. He thus gratefully writes of the change: "He took me by the hand, he drew me away from perdition's yawning gulf, directed my eye to himself, and opened to me the unfathomable abyss of his loving heart." He seemed to be drawn into closer fellowship with God as youth ripened into manhood, and to live, as it were, on the heavenly confines as manhood fruited in a serene and cloudless old age. At the age of twenty-seven, he dedicated all his resources and energies to the cause of Christ, writing the dedication in his own blood. "God graciously called me," he says, "out of the world, and granted me the desire to belong to him, and to be willing to follow him. I long for eternity that I may suitably glorify him for it."

When he was thirty years of age, a great spiritual awakening was experienced at Muhlheim, and although Tersteegen shrank from public notice, he was prevailed upon to address the people on themes relating to religious experience. He began to preach in private houses, but was soon compelled to enter upon more public labors. He gave up secular employments altogether, and devoted his whole time to religious instruction and to the poor. His house became famous as the Pilgrims' Cottage, and was visited not only by the most eminent Christians of Germany, but by multitudes of people from foreign lands. Thus spending his time in communion with God and in humble charities, and speaking to the spiritually-minded people who flocked to visit him, of the consolations of his own luminous experience, and of the new discoveries that grace was constantly making to his soul, beloved at home and revered and respected in foreign lands, his life drew near a triumphant exit, which took place, April 3, 1769. He lived an ascetic life in his best years, practising austerities, that no physical impediment might shut out the heavenly light or hinder the work of the Holy Spirit in comforming his soul to the will of God. He produced one hundred religious poems and spiritual songs, some of the best of which Wesley translated, and whose authorship is attributed to Wesley in most American collections of hymns.

The following is a very literal translation of Tersteegen's hymn before alluded to :

> God calling yet—and shall I never hearken ?
> But still earth's witcheries my spirit darken ;
> This passing life, these passing joys, all flying,
> And still my soul in dreamy slumbers lying.

God calling yet!—and I not yet arising?
So long his loving, faithful voice despising;
So falsely his unwearied care repaying;
He calls me still—and still I am delaying.

God calling yet! loud at my door he 's knocking,
And I, my heart, my ear, still firmer locking;
He still is ready, willing to receive me,
Is waiting now, but ah! he soon may leave me.

God calling yet!—and I no answer giving;
I dread his yoke, and am in bondage living.
Too long I linger, but not yet forsaken,
He calls me still—O my poor heart, awaken!

Oh, calling yet!—I can no longer tarry,
Nor to my God a heart divided carry;
Now, vain and giddy world, your spells are broken,
Sweeter than all! the voice of God hath spoken.

18. James Edmeston, a writer who seems to have sympathized deeply with piety in early childhood, was a London architect, and was born in 1791. He was a member of the Church of England. He wrote a collection of hymns for cottagers, which was followed by one hundred hymns for Sunday-schools. Many of his hymns were written week by week, to be read at the family devotions at his own home on Sunday morning. He was a friend of Mrs. Lake. The following favorite hymn is his:

LITTLE travellers Zionward,
Each one entering into rest,
In the kingdom of your Lord,
In the mansions of the blest;

> There to welcome Jesus waits,
>   Gives the crown his followers win;
> Lift your heads, ye golden gates,
>   Let the little travellers in.

> Who are they whose little feet,
>   Pacing life's dark journey through,
> Now have reached that heavenly seat
>   They had ever kept in view?
> " I, from Greenland's frozen land;"
>   " I, from India's sultry plain;"
> " I, from Afric's barren sand;"
>   " I, from islands of the main."

> " All our earthly journey passed,
>   Every tear and pain gone by,
> Here together met at last
>   At the portal of the sky,
> Each the welcome 'Come' awaits,
>   Conquerors over death and sin."
> Lift your heads, ye golden gates,
>   Let the little travellers in.

19. " Land in sight!" said John Adams, when dying. He was one of the mutineers of the " Bounty." He had dwelt on Pitcairn Island for forty years, building up a religious community in that " Paradise of the Pacific."

" Are you happy?" asked one who stood by his death-bed.

" Rounding the cape into the harbor," was the jubilant answer.

Nearer drew the saintly man to the celestial prospects; calmer became the haven.

" Let go the anchor," he exclaimed, and the Christian pioneer was no more.

This religious experience became the subject of the following Sunday-school hymn:

LAND ahead! its fruits are waving
· O'er the hills of fadeless green;
And the living waters laving
Shores where heavenly forms are seen.
CHORUS—Rocks and storms I 'll fear no more,
When on that eternal shore;
Drop the anchor! furl the sail!
I am safe within the veil.

Onward, bark! the cape I 'm rounding;
See, the blessed wave their hands;
Hear the harps of God resounding
From the bright immortal bands.—CHO.

There let go the anchor, riding
On this calm and silvery bay;
Seaward fast the tide is gliding,
Shores in sunlight stretch away.—CHO.

Now we 're safe from all temptation,
All the storms of life are past;
Praise the Rock of our salvation,
We are safe at home at last.—CHO.

20. The author of the following hymn, which is one of those recent productions which seem to be growing in the affections of the church, is Rev. J. H. Gilmore, now a professor in Rochester University, New York. He gives the following experience, as associated with its origin:

"I believe myself to be the author of 'He leadeth me.' Further, it was written in Philadelphia. I had made a talk at the Wednesday evening lecture of the First Baptist church, on the twenty-third Psalm; and, while a few of us were developing the subject a little farther in Deacon Watson's parlor, I jotted the hymn down in pencil precisely as it now stands—save that the refrain has since been added by another hand—and passed the paper to my wife, who sent it, without my knowledge, to the 'Watchman and Reflector.'

"The first time that I knew it had found its way into the hymn-books, was on the day on which I first entered the Second Baptist chapel in Rochester, to take a view of the surroundings before appearing before the church as a candidate. 'What do they sing in their social meetings?' I queried; and the 'Devotional Hymn and Tune Book' opened, of its own accord, to my own hymn, 'He leadeth me.'"

> HE leadeth me! Oh, blessed thought,
> Oh, words with heavenly comfort fraught;
> Whate'er I do, where'er I be,
> Still 't is God's hand that leadeth me!
>> He leadeth me! he leadeth me!
>> By his own hand he leadeth me;
>> His faithful follower I would be,
>> For by his hand he leadeth me.
>
> Sometimes 'mid scenes of deepest gloom,
> Sometimes where Eden's bowers bloom,
> By waters still, o'er troubled sea—
> Still 't is His hand that leadeth me!
>> He leadeth me, etc.
>
> Lord, I would clasp thy hand in mine,
> Nor ever murmur nor repine—
> Content, whatever lot I see,
> Since 't is my God that leadeth me.
>> He leadeth me, etc.

And when my task on earth is done,
When, by thy grace, the victory's won,
E'en death's cold wave I will not flee,
Since God through Jordan leadeth me.
　　He leadeth me, etc.

21. The song, " I am so glad that our Father in Heaven," by Mr. P. P. Bliss, an American composer, is very popular in Scotland as well as in America, and has been a leading tone in the services of the recent great revivals across the sea. It was suggested to Mr. Bliss by hearing the chorus,

" Oh, how I love Jesus."

The thought came to him, " I have sung long enough of my poor love to Christ, and now I will sing of his love for me." Under the inspiration of this thought, he wrote,

I AM so glad that our Father in heaven
Tells of his love in the book he has given;
Wonderful things in the Bible I see,
This is the dearest—that Jesus loves me.

Though I forget him, and wander away,
Kindly he follows wherever I stray;
Back to his dear, loving arms would I flee,
When I remember that Jesus loves me.

Oh, if there's only one song I can sing,
When in his beauty I see the great King,
This shall my song in eternity be—
Oh, what a wonder that Jesus loves me.

22. The song, " I gave my Life for thee," by Miss F. R. Havergal, was probably suggested by a German

motto under a picture of "Christ on the Cross."   It is
said that Count Zinzendorf owed his early Christian
experience to this motto, which brought vividly before
his young mind his obligations to Christ :

> I GAVE my life for thee,
>   My precious blood I shed,
> That thou might'st ransomed be
>   And quickened from the dead.
> I gave my life for thee :
> What hast thou given for me ?
>
> My Father's house of light,
>   My rainbow-circled throne,
> I left for earthly night,
>   For wanderings sad and lone ;
> I left it all for thee ;
> Hast thou left aught for me ?
>
> And I have brought to thee,
>   Down from my home above,
> Salvation full and free,
>   My pardon and my love.
> Great gifts I brought to thee ;
> What hast thou brought to me ?
>
> Oh ! let thy life be given,
>   Thy years for me be spent,
> World-fetters all be riven,
>   And joy with suffering blent.
> I gave myself for thee ;
> Give thou thyself to me.

V. SEAMEN'S HYMNS.

1. *FIERCE WAS THE WILD BILLOW.*
2. *JESUS, LOVER OF MY SOUL.*
3. *WHEN THROUGH THE TORN SAIL.*
4. *'LISTED IN THE CAUSE OF SIN.*
5. *I HEAR THE TEMPEST'S AWFUL SOUND.*

ORIGIN OF SEAMEN'S HYMNS.

THE principal seamen's hymn of the early church was that of St. Anatolius. It has lately been introduced into modern psalmody, being one of the happiest translations of Dr. John Mason Neale. Dr. Neale has not only clearly given the sense of the original, but has preserved the part of the Nicene creed—the "God of God," "Light of Light," and "Truth of Truth"—which it repeats. Its inspiration may have been drawn from the storms that beset the church, or from the tempests that darkened the Ionian seas.

FIERCE was the wild billow,
   Dark was the night;
Oars labored heavily,
   Foam glimmered white;
Mariners trembled,
   Peril was nigh:
Then said the God of God,
   "Peace! it is I."

Ridge of the mountain wave,
   Lower thy crest!
Wail of Euroclydon, -
   Be thou at rest!
Peril can none be,
   Sorrow must fly,
When saith the Light of Light,
   "Peace! it is I."

> Jesus, deliverer!
>   Come thou to me;
> Soothe thou my voyaging
>   Over life's sea.
> Thou, when the storm of death
>   Roars, sweeping by,
> Whisper, O Truth of Truth,
>   " Peace! it is I."

The origin of the best known sailors' hymns is interesting, most of them being produced after perilous experiences at sea. Perhaps no hymn is more sung on the water than Charles Wesley's, beginning,

"Jesus, lover of my soul."

It was written in 1740, shortly after Wesley's return from America to England, and during the first stormy scenes of his itinerant preaching. Whether the figures in the first stanza were suggested by the storms of the Atlantic, which the writer had but recently encountered, or by the storms of human passion, we cannot say. But most of the sea hymns of Charles Wesley were but the unfoldings of actual experiences. In his journal on the Atlantic, he thus describes his spiritual conflicts and triumphs during a storm : " I prayed for power to pray, for faith in Jesus Christ, continually repeating his name, till I felt the virtue of it at last, and knew I abode under the shadow of the Almighty. The storm was at its height. At four o'clock, the ship made so much water, that the captain, finding it impossible otherwise to save her from sinking, cut down the mizen mast. In this dreadful moment, I bless God, I found comfort and hope, and

C.Wesley

such joy in finding I could hope as the world can neither
give nor take away. I had that conviction of the power
of God present with me, overruling fear, and raising me
above what I am by nature, as surpassed all rational evidence." On the storm subsiding, he wrote: "Towards
morning the sea heard and obeyed the divine voice,
'Peace, be still.' My first business to-day—may it be
the first business of all my days—was to offer up the
sacrifice of praise and thanksgiving."

> "All praise to the Lord,
>   Who rules with a word
>   Th' untractable sea."

Bishop Heber's matchless hymn beginning,

> "When through the torn sail
>   The wild tempest is streaming,"

was written after similar experiences. The bishop took
an affectionate interest in the humblest sailors during
his voyages. "Only to think," said a grateful seaman,
"of such a great man as the bishop coming between
decks to pray with such poor fellows as we."

> "O Jesus! once tossed
>   On the breast of the billow,
>   Aroused by the shriek
>   Of despair from thy pillow,
>   High now in thy glory,
>   The mariner cherish,
>   Who cries in his anguish,
>   'Lord, save, or we perish.'"

Many of our readers have doubtless seen in old hymn-
books a spirited hymn beginning with this singular
stanza :

> " 'Listed in the cause of sin,
>   Why should a good be evil ?
> Music, alas ! has too long been
>   Pressed to obey the devil."

The hymn is ascribed to Charles Wesley, and the quoted stanza must have struck the reader as a marked exception to the mellifluent numbers of this most careful and cultured lyrist. It was composed amid the roughest scenes of his itinerant preaching in Cornwall, when mobs set upon him in every town, among whom were the wreckers, a class of sea-robbers long passed away.

The Cornish seamen always loved to sing that hymn, and the Old Methodists of Cornwall delighted to tell the story of its origin.

" My father knew all about that hymn," said a Cornish man to a recent English writer. " Mr. C. Wesley had just begun a hymn in the open-air, intending to preach to the gathering crowd, when some half-drunken fellows came and struck up the tune of ' Nancy Dawson.' Between the hymn and their song it was sorry music, but the preacher's ear was quick enough to catch the metre of their song, and to master their tune there and then. He invited them to come again by-and-by, when he would be there and sing a song to their tune. They came and he gave out a new hymn made for the occasion. The merry tars seemed to enjoy the hymn more than their old song.

" A cheery thing," added the Cornishman, " it was to hear my father sing it, just as the old folks, he said, used to sing it. I used to sing it with him. He and I shall join again by-and-by, and ' Heaven be ours for ever.' "

The following stanzas exhibit the spirit of the hymn;

> " Come let us see if Jesus' love
> Will not as well inspire us ;
> This is the theme of those above :
> This upon earth shall fire us.
>
> " Say, if your hearts are tuned to sing,
> Is there a subject greater?
> Harmony all its strains may bring,
> But Jesus' name is sweeter.
>
> " Then let us in his praises join,
> Triumph in his salvation,
> Glory ascribe to love divine,
> Worship and adoration.
>
> " Heaven already is begun,
> Open to each believer ;
> Only believe and still go on,
> Heaven is ours for ever."

About one hundred and twenty years ago, there wandered among the palm groves of Sierra Leone, a young Englishman, who had fallen so low as to be shunned even by the rude traders on the coast, and by the African slaves. He had little clothing; he went hungry, and often was obliged to subsist upon roots. His life was not only stained with vice, but with viciousness in its most disgusting forms. He had a pious mother, and the memory of her counsels and prayers, like good angels, followed him in all of his wanderings. Escaping at last from the coast, he secured a passage for England.

During the homeward voyage the ship encountered a terrible storm. " I began to pray," he said. " I could not utter the prayer of faith. My prayer was like the cry of the ravens, which yet the Lord does not disdain to hear." The storm subsided, but the young man, sick at last of sin, continued to pray. God revealed his salvation to him on the ocean, and out of this deep experience, came the sailor's hymn, beginning,

> " I hear the tempest's awful sound,
>   I feel the vessel's quick rebound;
>   And fear might now my bosom fill,
>   But Jesus tells me, ' Peace ! be still.
>
> ' In this dread hour I cling to thee,
>   My Saviour crucified for me.
>   If that I perish be thy will,
>   In death, Lord, whisper, ' Peace ! be still.' "

That young man was John Newton, the rector of St. Woolnoth, London, the friend of Cowper, and the writer of a part of the Olney Hymns.

VI. INDIAN HYMNS.

INDIAN HYMNS.

In de dark wood, no Indian nigh,
Den me look heaben, and send up cry,
    Upon my knees so low.
Dat God on high, in shinee place,
See me in night, with teary face,
    De priest, he tell me so.

God send he angels take me care;
He come heself and hear my prayer,
    If inside heart do pray.
God see me now, he know me here.
He say, poor Indian, neber fear,
    Me wid you night and day.

So me lub God wid inside heart;
He fight for me, he take my part,
    He save my life before.
God lub poor Indian in de wood;
So me lub God, and dat be good;
    Me 'll praise him two times more.

When me be old, me head be gray,
Den he no lebe me, so he say:
    Me wid you till you die.
Den take me up to shinee place,
See white man, red man, black man's face,
    All happy 'like on high.

16

> Few days, den God will come to me,
> He knock off chains, he set me free,
>   Den take me up on high.
> Den Indian sing his praises blest,
> And lub and praise him wid de rest,
>   And neber, neber cry.

The above hymn, which may be found in different forms in old New England tracts and hymn-books, and which used to be sung in Methodist conference and prayer-meetings, in the same way that old slave-hymns and the "Jubilee Singers" refrains are sometimes sung now, was composed by William Apes, a converted Indian, who was born in Massachusetts in 1798. His father was a white man, but married an Indian descended from the family of King Philip, the Indian warrior, and the last of the Indian chiefs. His grandmother was the king's granddaughter, as he claimed, and was famous for her personal beauty. He caused his autobiography and religious experience to be published. The original hymn is quite long, and contains some singular and characteristic expressions.

In the early days of New England, before the Indian missions had been brought to an end by the sweeping away of the tribes, several fine hymns were composed by Indians, and were used in the churches. The best known is that beginning,

> "When shall we three meet again?"

It was composed by three Indians at the planting of a memorial pine on leaving Dartmouth College, where they

had been receiving a Christian education. The stanzas
which follow are particularly fine:

> " Though in distant lands we sigh,
> Parched beneath a burning sky,
> Though the deep between us rolls,
> Friendship shall unite our souls ;
> And in fancy's wide domain,
> There we three shall meet again.

> " When the dreams of life are fled,
> When its wasted lamps are dead,
> When in cold oblivion's shade
> Beauty, health, and strength are laid,
> Where immortal spirits reign,
> There we three shall meet again."

These Indians afterwards met in the same place and
composed another hymn, which is as beautiful and touching. It begins:

> " Parted many a toil-spent year,
> Pledged in youth to memory dear,
> Still to friendship's magnet true,
> We our social joys renew ;
> Bound by love's unsevered chain,
> Here on earth we meet again."

VII. RECENT HYMN-WRITERS AND THEIR HYMNS.

1. *FREDERICK WILLIAM FABER.*
2. *REV. JOHN KEBLE.*
3. *HORATIUS BONAR, D. D.*
4. *CHARLOTTE ELLIOTT.*
5. *SARAH FLOWER ADAMS.*
6. *PHŒBE CARY.*
7. *RAY PALMER, D. D.*
8. *REV. HENRY FRANCIS LYTE.*
9. *REV. JOHN HENRY NEWMAN.*

16*

RECENT HYMN-WRITERS AND THEIR HYMNS.

FABER.

FREDERICK WILLIAM FABER, the author of some of
the most finished, ornate, and peculiarly beautiful poems
of the present generation of hymn-writers, was born
in 1815, was early schooled at Harrow, and graduated
at Oxford, in 1836. He was a minister of the Established church for some ten years, but at the age of
thirty-one he became a communicant of the church of
Rome. After the change in his views, he established a
brotherhood of priests at London, and lived a somewhat
secluded and ascetic life. He died in 1863.

His hymns are flowers from both Catholic and Protestant soil, but are generally as liberal in spirit as they
are pure in diction and lofty in sentiment. He had
many religious doubts and conflicts, and his life, though
uneventful, was one of peculiar experiences. He died in
the prime of manhood, yet lived to say :

> "A weary actor, I would fain
> Be quit of my long part,
> The burden of unquiet life
> Lies heavy on my heart."

Both of the hymns which we give, are from a collection of Faber's poems, called "Oratory Hymns," and

are colored by his own religious feelings. They indicate his unrest, and his expectation of peace at last. They are found in both Protestant and Catholic collections.

I.

HARK ! hark, my soul ! angelic songs are swelling
  O'er earth's green fields and ocean's wave-beat shore;
How sweet the truth those blessed strains are telling
  Of that new life when sin shall be no more !
      Angels of Jesus,
        Angels of light,
      Singing to welcome
        The pilgrims of the night.

Onward we go, for still we hear them singing,
  "Come, weary souls, for Jesus bids you come;"
And through the dark, its echoes sweetly ringing,
  The music of the gospel leads us home.
      Angels of Jesus, etc.

Far, far away, like bells at evening pealing,
  The voice of Jesus sounds o'er land and sea,
And laden souls by thousands meekly stealing
  Kind Shepherd, turn their weary steps to thee.
      Angels of Jesus, etc.

Rest comes at length, though life be long and dreary,
  The day must dawn, and darksome night be past;
All journeys end in welcome to the weary,
  And heaven, the heart's true home, will come at last.
      Angels of Jesus, etc.

Angels, sing on ! your faithful watches keeping;
  Sing us sweet fragments of the songs above;
Till morning's joy shall end the night of weeping,
  And life's long night shall break in endless love.
      Angels of Jesus, etc.

II.

O Paradise, O Paradise!
  Who doth not crave for rest?
Who would not seek the happy land
  Where they that loved are blest?
    Where loyal hearts and true
      Stand ever in the light,
    All rapture through and through,
      In God's most holy sight.

O Paradise, O Paradise!
  The world is growing old;
Who would not be at rest and free
  Where love is never cold?
    Where loyal hearts and true, etc.

O Paradise, O Paradise!
  'T is weary waiting here;
I long to be where Jesus is,
  To feel, to see him near;
    Where loyal hearts and true, etc.

O Paradise, O Paradise!
  I want to sin no more,
I want to be as pure on earth
  As on thy spotless shore;
    Where loyal hearts and true, etc.

O Paradise, O Paradise!
  I greatly long to see
The special place my dearest Lord
  In love prepares for me;
    Where loyal hearts and true
      Stand ever in the light,
    All rapture through and through,
      In God's most holy sight.

KEBLE.

Sun of my soul! thou Saviour dear,
It is not night if thou be near:
Oh, may no earth-born cloud arise
To hide thee from thy servant's eyes.

When the soft dews of kindly sleep
My wearied eyelids gently steep,
Be my last thought, how sweet to rest
For ever on my Saviour's breast.

Abide with me from morn till eve,
For without thee I cannot live;
Abide with me when night is nigh,
For without thee I dare not die.

If some poor wandering child of thine
Have spurned, to-day, the voice divine,
Now, Lord, the gracious work begin;
Let him no more lie down in sin.

Watch by the sick; enrich the poor
With blessings from thy boundless store:
Be every mourner's sleep to-night
Like infant's slumbers pure and light.

Come near and bless us when we wake,
Ere through the world our way we take;
Till in the ocean of thy love
We lose ourselves in heaven above.   .

This hymn is from Keble's " Christian Year," a book
that embodies many choice Christian experiences, which
have been recognized with gratitude by the universal
church, although especially written for those whose worship follows the set forms of the Church of England.
Mr. Keble lived a quiet, retired life, and drank from
spiritual fountains in secluded places; but his rare gifts

were devoted to the service of others, and he has won by the affectionate purity and the deep spiritual insight of his poetic writings, a large place in the heart of the Christian world.

We condense from an English periodical some account of his uneventful yet ever-fruitful life.

As beautiful and venerable a reputation as any treasured up in the annals of the English church, is that of the author of the " Christian Year," for upwards of thirty years vicar of Hursley and rector of Otterbourne. It is not too much to say that when he breathed his last at seventy-four years of age, in the spring of 1866, he not only did so, within the recognition of men of every kind of Christian belief, in the odor of sanctity, but that he had enjoyed already for half a century what was thenceforth embalmed by death into an exquisite memory, the blended fame of a saint and a poet. His whole life, it may be said quite truly, was passed within the shadow of the sanctuary. For fifty years together, his father, who survived until his ninetieth year, was the vicar of Coln Saint Aldwyn. There it was, under the roof-beams of the old parsonage, that John Keble was born, on the 25th April, 1792.

On the 20th May, 1813, Keble had taken his degree of M. A. Parochial work began for him immediately upon his ordination. It ceased only with his life—fifty years afterwards.

In 1823 Keble withdrew from a conspicuous and lucrative position as tutor and examiner at the University of Oxford, and retired to the seclusion of Fairford, entering upon duties as curate of three small parishes; an act of Christian humility whose golden rewards were yet unseen. The three curacies together did not include a population of three thousand. The entire receipts accruing to him in connection with them all, did not amount to more than about £100 a year. He was happy in his surroundings, however, and in his avocations, but above all thrice happy in his sacred calling. Covertly, too, he was wandering all this while, since as far back as in 1819, in a green and flowery pleasaunce of his own, in which his serene fancy made a sunshine in the shadiest place, and where his spirit secretly heard the plash and tinkling of celestial fountains. Little by little, one by one, he was composing at Oxford, at Fairford, by the Isis, by the Coln, in the gardens, in the meadows, unknown except to the inner circle of his most intimate friends, those beautiful lyrics which, under the title of the " Christian Year," when completed, some four years after the date at which we have arrived, sprang at once into such resplendent celebrity, achieving a success that has been maintained undiminished ever since, and that is simply and absolutely unparalleled.

Another temptation was held out to Keble early in 1824. William Hart Coleridge had just then been selected to fill one of the two newly-created sees in the West Indies, as Bishop of Barbadoes. A couple of archdeaconries were in his gift, each worth £2,000 a year, and one of these he urgently pressed upon Keble's acceptance. Dazzled though he may have been for a passing moment by this offer to advance him *per saltum* to the position of archdeacon of Barbadoes, the gifted but simple-minded curate of Southrop, Eastleach, and Burthorpe declined it, nevertheless, unhesitatingly. His home-ties, his father's increasing age and infirmities, his tender regard for his two sisters—his different affection for whom he prettily typified by speaking of his "wife" Margaret and his "sweetheart" Mary Anne—held him securely, by preference, to his lowlier position as a working curate in Gloucestershire. The song-bird that soars highest towards heaven among the dews and sunbeams, makes its nest, by preference, not in an eyrie or in the tree-top, but among the grass or between the furrows of a cornfield.

During eight years altogether—that is, from 1819 to 1827—Keble had been gradually preparing what at length made its appearance as his masterpiece: "The Christian Year." It had germinated, grown, and expanded under his hand very gradually and at first almost imperceptibly. It was with no affected reluctance that he at length, yielding to the importunity of those immediately around him, consented to its appearance. His father, who was every day, it seemed, descending nearer and nearer towards the entrance of the Valley of the Shadow, expressed an eager solicitude to witness its publication. The manuscript passed into the printer's hands, and the proofs, one by one, found their way to Fairford for the author's timid and ever-wincing correction. His own preference would have been that they should have appeared posthumously. Against his judgment, however, it was decided otherwise by those to whose opinions he deferred. On the 23d June, 1827, the "Christian Year" was first published. It stole its way into the public heart instantly. It influenced all it came across with a spell of fascination. Its success was emotional rather than a matter of reasoning and of criticism. Keble's readers were like those who listened to some sweet and delicious melody chanted by a singer who was hidden from view in the twilight. Their hearts were moved, their nerves thrilled, their eyes glistened, they were charmed by a voice that was at once new and yet familiar. Before the December of that year was out, a second edition had been required. In 1828, the third made its appearance. One followed another in rapid succession. When but a little more than a quarter of a century had elapsed, forty-three editions had been exhausted, 108,000 copies had already even then passed into circulation. Before its author's life was completed and crowned by a death so serene and calm that it was a veritable euthanasia, the astonish ing number of ninety-two editions of the " Christian Year" had passed from the hands of his publishers.

HORATIUS BONAR, D. D.

HORATIUS BONAR, whose hymns are among the sweet minor tones that are yearly growing in the love of the church, was born in Edinburgh, in 1808, and was educacated at Edinburgh University. Religious impressions were early made upon his mind, and his mental conflicts ended in the peace of Christ :

> " I heard the voice of Jesus say,
>   'Come unto me and rest :
>   Lay down, thou weary one, lay down
>   Thy head upon my breast.'

I came to Jesus as I was,
  Weary, and worn, and sad,
I found in him a resting-place,
  And he has made me glad.

"I heard the voice of Jesus say,
  'I am this dark world's light,
Look unto me, thy morn shall rise
  And all thy day be bright.'
I looked to Jesus, and I found
  In him my star, my sun:
And in that light of life I 'll walk,
  Till all my journey's done."

In his early manhood he felt an inward inspiration to become a minister, and to give his life to others, and he obeyed the voice speaking within him, and was ordained at Kelso in 1837.

He entered upon the work of carrying the Word of Life to others, with an unusual ardor and unsparing zeal. The young minister began to publish tracts and hymns, on subjects connected with his religious work and inward experience. His Kelso tracts began to appear in 1839. One of these entitled "Believe and Live" attained the circulation of 750,000 copies. Christ and the love of Christ were the themes of his sermons, his tracts, and his songs:

"I lay my wants on Jesus;
  All fulness dwells in him;
He heals all my diseases,
  He doth my soul redeem.
I lay my griefs on Jesus,
  My burdens and my cares;
He from them all releases,
  He all my sorrow shares.

> " I rest my soul on Jesus,
>   This weary soul of mine ;
> His right hand me embraces,
>   I on his breast recline.
> I love the name of Jesus,
>   Immanuel, Christ, the Lord ;
> Like fragrance on the breezes
>   His name abroad is poured."

He was an advocate of the Free Church of Scotland, and was one of the glorious band of ministers who renounced their livings, when, in 1843, the church threw off the thraldom of state.   He has published several volumes of sacred poetry, the best known of which is " Hymns of Faith and Hope."   As a lyric poet he has hardly a superior.   The following—an expression of personal experience—is perhaps one of his best-known and most expressive hymns :

> Fade, fade each earthly joy ;
>   Jesus is mine !
> Break, every tender tie ;
>   Jesus is mine !
> Jesus alone can bless ;
> Dark is the wilderness ;
> Earth has no resting-place ;
>   Jesus is mine !
>
> Tempt not my soul away ;
>   Jesus is mine !
> Here would I ever stay ;
>   Jesus is mine !
> Perishing things of clay,
> Born but for one brief day,
> Pass from my heart away,
>   Jesus is mine !

> Farewell, ye dreams of night,
>   Jesus is mine!
> Lost in this dawning bright,
>   Jesus is mine!
> All that my soul has tried
> Left but a dismal void;
> Jesus has satisfied;
>   Jesus is mine!
>
> Farewell, mortality:
>   Jesus is mine!
> Welcome, eternity:
>   Jesus is mine!
> Welcome, O loved and blest;
> Welcome, sweet scenes of rest;
> Welcome, my Saviour's breast:
>   Jesus is mine!

CHARLOTTE ELLIOTT.

THIS hymn writer, to whom we have made a brief reference elsewhere, in connection with the hymn, beginning " Just as I am, without one plea," was the third daughter of Charles Elliott, Esq., of Clapham and Brighton, England, and a granddaughter of Rev. John Venn, a name conspicuous in the great religious awakening of the last century. She was born on March 18, 1789. She lived to extreme old age, but was for the greater part of her life an invalid. She died Sept. 22, 1871.

She was highly educated and accomplished, and, possessing a warm social nature, she eagerly sought the companionship of gay society in an interval of restored health in early life. In the midst of this gay opening, she fell ill, and her mind became exercised about religion.

After great inward conflicts, and much reading and praying, she was led to an insight of the way of life, and was enabled to accept Christ as her Saviour and Deliverer, thus fulfilling in spirit the sentiment which she afterwards embodied in her immortal hymn :

Just as I am, without one plea,
But that thy blood was shed for me,
And that thou bid'st me come to thee,
  O Lamb of God, I come.

Just as I am, and waiting not
To rid my soul of one dark blot,
To thee, whose blood can cleanse each spot,
  O Lamb of God, I come.

Just as I am, though tossed about
With many a conflict, many a doubt,
Fightings and fears within, without,
  O Lamb of God, I come.

Just as I am, poor, wretched, blind—
Sight, riches, healing of the mind,
Yea, all I need, in thee to find,
  O Lamb of God, I come.

Just as I am, thou wilt receive,
Wilt welcome, pardon, cleanse, relieve;
Because thy promise I believe,
  O Lamb of God, I come.

Just as I am, thy love unknown,
Has broken every barrier down;
Now to be thine, yea, thine alone,
  O Lamb of God, I come.

Just as I am, of that free love
The breadth, length, depth, and height, to prove,
Here for a season, then above—
  O Lamb of God, I come.

She became a close student of the Bible, and devoted the whole of her time and talent to religious work. She loved poetry, and possessed the gift of expressing her thoughts and feelings in verse, and this gift she also dedicated to the service of God.

In 1823, a series of family bereavements led her to a higher religious life, and, under the inspiration of glowing conceptions of the love of Christ, and a conscientious zeal for the conversion of souls, she joined a district society, under the direction of Mrs. Fry and Rev. Edward Irving. She became an active worker for the church, and was also on intimate terms with Wilberforce, and an advocate of his schemes of philanthropy.

In 1829, she became a chronic invalid. The lesson of resignation was at first hard to learn ; but she was patient and teachable, and was brought through suffering to experience those heavenly dispositions of mind that make one strong in weakness, and bring to the soul the luminous discoveries of Christian faith. She writes of this experience :

"Oh, many hard struggles and apparently fruitless ones it has cost me to become resigned to the appointments of my Heavenly Father. *But the struggle is now over.* He knows, and he alone, what it is, day after day, hour after hour, to fight against bodily feelings of almost overpowering weakness, languor and exhaustion, to resolve not to yield to slothfulness, depression, and instability, such as the body causes me to long to indulge, but to rise every morning determined to take for my motto: ' If any man will come after Me, let him deny himself,

take up his cross daily and follow Me.'" This discipline
and resignation became the subject of one of her most
loved hymns :

> My God, my Father, while I stray
> Far from my home, on life's rough way,
> O teach me from my heart to say,
>   "Thy will be done."
>
> Though dark my path, and sad my lot,
> Let me be still and murmur not,
> Or breathe the prayer divinely taught,
>   " Thy will be done."
>
> What though in lonely grief I sigh
> For friends beloved no longer nigh,
> Submissive still would I reply,
>   "Thy will be done."
>
> If thou shouldst call me to resign
> What most I prize—if ne'er was mine ;
> I only yield thee what is thine—
>   " Thy will be done."
>
> Let but my fainting heart be blest
> With thy sweet Spirit for its guest,
> My God, to thee I leave the rest:
>   " Thy will be done."
>
> Renew my will from day to day,
> Blend it with thine, and take away
> All that now makes it hard to say,
>   " Thy will be done."

The larger number of her hymns were published under the following circumstances: In 1834, she became
acquainted with Miss Kiernan, a benevolent woman of
Dublin, who, in her last illness, began the preparation of
a hymn-book for invalids.   After her death, the work was
put into the hands of Charlotte Elliott to finish.   It was

a work in which she was in sympathy, and peculiarly fitted to complete. She added a large number of hymns of her own composition, among them that beginning "Just as I am." The sale of this collection of hymns reached nearly 20,000 copies.

The hymn "Just as I am" was printed, unknown to the writer, on leaflets, for gratuitous distribution, and her physician brought one of these to her, not knowing that she had written it. "I know," he said, "that this will please you." It did indeed please her to know that in her own helplessness her life was helpful to others.

She lived to be an octogenarian. Her last manifestation of consciousness on her sick-bed was when her sister read to her the Scripture lesson on the morning of her death : "Thine eyes shall see the King in his beauty." She was observed to raise her eyes to heaven, and a sudden glow of joy seemed to illumine her countenance.

SARAH FLOWER ADAMS.

THE AUTHOR OF "NEARER, MY GOD, TO THEE."

PERHAPS no hymn, since the publication of Perronet's "All hail the power of Jesus' name," in 1785, has received so wide and deserving a popularity as that beginning, "Nearer, my God, to thee." It finds a place in all collections of hymns in the English tongue, and is a favorite alike in Trinitarian and Unitarian churches. It has been translated into many languages, and has followed the triumphs of the Gospel in heathen lands. It is the best metrical expression of the desire for a more intimate spiritual ac-

quaintance with God, and the riches of his grace, that
we have in modern psalmody. It is a fresh and touching expression of the same yearning aspirations toward
God that we prize in Cowper's " Oh, for a closer walk
with God," which it succeeds in popular favor. It expresses a willingness to know God through the discipline of affliction ; to descend into the valleys in the
ascent of that spiritual mountain whose summit is everlasting light.

Its imagery embraces the associations of one of
the most sublime and interesting religious experiences
recorded in the early Hebrew Scriptures—Jacob's vision
at Luz. "And he lighted upon a certain place," says
the Scripture of Jacob's wanderings, "and tarried there
all night, because the sun was set ; and he took of the
stones of that place, and put them for his pillows, and
lay down in that place to sleep. And he dreamed, and
behold a ladder set up on the earth, and the top of it
reached to heaven ; and behold the angels of God as-
cending and descending on it." The hymn almost literally reproduces this delightful passage :

<blockquote>
" Though like the wanderer,
  The sun gone down,
Darkness be over me,
  My rest a stone,
Yet in my dreams I 'd be
Nearer, my God, to thee,
  Nearer to thee."
</blockquote>

The scriptural account of the waking of Jacob on the
morning after the vision is as vividly brought to mind in
the figures used in the fourth stanza of the hymn :

> " Then with my waking thoughts
>   Bright with thy praise,
> Out of my stony grief
>   Bethel I 'll raise ;
> So by my woes to be
> Nearer, my God, to thee,
>   Nearer to thee."

Mrs. Sarah Flower Adams, the author of the hymn, was the younger of two daughters of Benjamin Flower, an English wiriter and editor. She was born in 1805. Her mother, a lady of culture, refined feelings and sentiments, died early in life.

Her elder sister's name was Eliza. The strongest attachment existed between the two sisters ; both possessed the fine feelings of their mother, and were fond of books, music, poetry, and art. Their æsthetic tastes discovered themselves in childhood, and girlhood to them was a glowing season of aspiration and expectancy. Eliza turned her attention to music and musical composition, and her sister to religious poetry. They were Unitarian in their church relations, but their piety was gauged by devotional feeling and high religious attainments, rather than by denominational requirements or any sectarian views.

"Eliza Flower," says a critic, "attained a higher rank in musical composition, than before her time had been reached by any of her sex. Sarah Flower made the composition of poetry her occupation, while her sister pursued her musical studies. In 1834, she married William Bridges Adams, an eminent engineer, and a contributor to the best periodical literature In 1841, she published a dramatic poem in five acts, entitled, " Vivia Perpetua," in which she portrays the religious life, sufferings, strong faith, and endurance, of the early martyrs.

The hymn " Nearer, my God, to thee," was a record of her own religious experience, and was written as a memorial of answered prayer, probably without any expectation that it would be of public service. It was furnished with thirteen other hymns to Charles Fox's collection of " Hymns and Anthems," published in London, in 1841.

The cares of married life in nowise abated her early attachment to her equally gifted sister. Regarding " Vivia Perpetua" as the fruit of their joint aspirations and studies, she dedicates it to her sister in some lines in which occurs the following tender sentiment:

> " In thy content, I win a wreath more bright
> Than earth's wide garden ever could supply;
> Ah, me! I think me still how poor a strain!
> And fly for refuge to thy love again."

Her sister's health beginning to decline and evidences of pulmonary consumption appearing, she devoted herself to the invalid's room with unceasing watchfulness and self-forgetful care. Eliza Flower died in 1847. Mrs. Adams never recovered from the shock of the separation. Her religious aspirations, always strong, seemed now to receive a heavenly impulse. Her health gradually declined, and, in 1849, two years after her sister's death, she too peacefully fell asleep.

In her hymn, she gives expression to the following jubilant expectation :

> " Or if on joyful wing,
>   Cleaving the sky,
> Sun, moon, and stars forgot,
>   Upward I fly,
> Still all my song shall be,
> Nearer my God to thee,
>   Nearer to thee."

This hope seems to have been almost literally fulfilled in her death. We are told that "almost her last breath burst into unconscious song."

The following hymn by Mrs. Adams seems to have been written in the same spirit as " Nearer, my God, to Thee." It was sung at her funeral :

> " He sendeth sun, he sendeth shower,
> Alike they 're needful to the flower ;
> And joys and tears alike are sent
> To give the soul fit nourishment ;
> As comes to me or cloud or sun,
> Father, thy will, not mine, be done.

> " Oh, ne'er will I at life repine,
> Enough that thou hast made it mine ;
> Where falls the shadow cold in death,
> I yet will sing with fearless breath ;
> As comes to me or shade or sun,
> Father, thy will, not mine be done."

The last stanza seems prophetic when we recall the song of praise that trembled on her dying lips.

PHŒBE CARY.

THE grave has but recently closed· over Phœbe **Cary**, the author of the following hymn, and one of the sweetest

American poets. She possessed a loving and trustful soul, and her life was an honor to true womanhood and a blessing to the poor. She had to struggle with hardship and poverty in her early years ; " I have cried in the street because I was poor," she said in her prosperous years, " and the poor always seem nearer to me than the rich."

She was a member of the Church of the Pilgrims in New York, during the pastorate of Dr. Cheever. In her last years she attended the Church of the Stranger (Dr. Deems') in the same city. Her early years were passed in a simple rural home in the West, but after obtaining reputation as a writer she removed to New York where she was greatly loved for her modest worth, and where she became a quiet but influential leader in literary society.

The hymn by which she is best known, and which will probably survive her other published works, is entitled " Nearer Home."

> ONE sweetly solemn thought
>   Comes to me o'er and o'er,
> I am nearer home to-day,
>   Then I ever have been before.
>
> Nearer my Father's house,
>   Where the many mansions be,
> Nearer the great white throne,
>   Nearer the crystal sea.
>
> Nearer the bound of life,
>   Where we lay our burdens down,
> Nearer leaving the cross
>   Nearer gaining the crown.

> But lying darkly between,
> 　Winding down through shades of night,
> Is the silent unknown stream,
> 　That leads at last to the light.
>
> Closer and closer my steps
> 　Come to the dread abysm,
> Closer death to my lips
> 　Presses the awful chrism.
>
> Oh, if my mortal feet,
> 　Have almost gained the brink,
> If it be that I 'm nearer home,
> 　Even to-day than I think,
>
> Father, perfect my trust,
> 　Let my spirit feel in death
> That her feet are firmly set
> 　On the rock of living faith.

The author did not set a high intellectual value upon this composition at the time it was written, and she was surprised to. find it outgrowing in popularity all of her more carefully penned and elaborate productions.

It was a hymn of heart-experience. She thus gives an account of its origin in a letter to an esteemed friend :

" I enclose the hymn for you. It was written eighteen years ago (1852) in your own house. I composed it in the the little back third story bedroom, one Sunday morning, after coming from church ; and it makes me very happy to think that any word I could say has done any good in the world."

In its original form the hymn was very irregular and not adapted to be sung. Metrical versions have therefore been arranged by compilers, none of them quite satisfactory. The following is one of the best:

> ONE sweetly solemn thought
>   Comes to me o'er and o'er:
> Nearer my going home am I
>   Than e'er I 've been before;
>
> Nearer my Father's house
>   Where many mansions be,
> Nearer the throne where Jesus reigns,
>   Nearer the crystal sea.
>
> Nearer the bound of life,
>   Where we lay our burdens down,
> Leaving the cross of heavy grief
>   Wearing the starry crown.
>
> Nearer the hidden stream
>   Winding through shades of night,
> Rolling its cold, dark waves between
>   Me and the world of light.
>
> Jesus, to thee I cling;
>   Strengthen my arm of faith,
> Stand near me when my wayworn feet
>   Pass through the stream of death.

Miss Cary died at Newport, R. I., Monday, July 31, 1871. Her remains were interred from New York, in Greenwood Cemetery, and this hymn was sung at her funeral.

The following pleasing incident has been told of the influence of Miss Cary's hymn in a foreign land:

Two Americans, one a young man, the other over forty, were drinking and playing at cards in a gambling house in China. While the older one was shuffling the cards, the younger began to hum, and finally sung in a low tone, but quite unconsciously, this hymn. The older one threw down the cards on the floor and said,

"Harry, where did you learn that hymn?"

"What hymn?"

"Why that one you have been singing."

The young man said he did not know what he had been singing. But when the older one repeated some of the lines, he said they were learned in the Sunday-school.

"Come, Harry," said the older one, "come, here's what I've won from you. As for me, as God sees me, I have played my last game, and drank my last bottle. I have misled you, Harry, and I am sorry for it. Give me your hand, my boy, and say that, for old America's sake, if for no other, you will quit this infernal business."

Col. Russel H. Conwell, of Boston, who was then visiting China, and was an eye-witness of the scene, says that the reformation was a permanent one.

————+————

RAY PALMER.

My faith looks up to thee,
Thou Lamb of Calvary:
　　Saviour divine,
Now hear me while I pray;
Take all my guilt away;
Oh let me from this day
　　Be wholly thine.

May thy rich grace impart
Strength to my fainting heart:
　　My zeal inspire;
As thou hast died for me,
O may my love to thee
Pure warm and changeless be—
　　A living fire.

18*

> While life's dark maze I tread,
> And griefs around me spread,
>   Be thou my Guide;
> Bid darkness turn to day;
> Wipe sorrow's tears away,
> Nor let me ever stray
>   From thee aside.
>
> When ends life's transient dream;
> When death's cold, sullen stream
>   Shall o'er me roll;
> Blest Saviour, then, in love
> Fear and distrust remove;
> Oh bear me safe above,
>   A ransomed soul.

This hymn was written by Dr. Ray Palmer, about the year 1830. He was a student at the time, preparing for the ministry. His health was very poor, and his worldly prospects clouded. He felt that the world could promise him nothing, and in an hour of despondency, the young student turned, as his only help and resource, to the promises of God. Comforted in spirit by Him "to whom all things are possible," he tells his experience and expresses his hope for the future in these lines.

The hymn at first seems not to have been intended for publication. It was carried about in the writer's pocket for a considerable time. Meeting Dr. Lowell Mason, one day, he was asked to furnish a hymn for a tune then written or about to be composed. Dr. Palmer, then about twenty-two years of age, drew forth the poem he had written under these severe trials and interesting circumstances, and it was soon after published with the music by Dr. Mason.

HENRY FRANCIS LYTE,

THE AUTHOR OF "ABIDE WITH ME."

In the year 1818, an Episcopal minister at Marazion, England, distinguished for his brilliant gifts, culture, and poetic tastes, was sent for by a neighboring clergyman, who felt that he was dying. The interview was a most solemn and impressive one.

"I am about to die," said the invalid, "and I am unpardoned and quite unprepared."

The two clergymen took their Bibles, and read together the writings of St. Paul, in search of the way of spiritual peace. Prayer brought to each the desired blessing, the precious love of Christ. The latter died in triumph, and the former entered upon his mission in life with new views, new consolations, and a new zeal, consecrating all his powers, his social and poetic gifts to religion.

This clergyman was Henry Francis Lyte. He was educated at Trinity College, Dublin, where his first poetic gifts appeared, and where he won a reputation as a scholar, competing successfully on three occasions for the prize offered for the best English poem.

After his conversion, the high aspirations of literary eminence that had formed a part of the dreams of his youth, changed. Gentle and childlike in spirit, he desired to serve God by laboring for the poor.

In the year 1823, he entered upon the perpetual curacy of Dower Brixham, Devon, which he held till his death, laboring among a poor, rough, seafaring population. These experiences and changes in life are expressed in his much-loved hymn :

> "Jesus, I my cross have taken,
>   All to leave and follow thee."

Here, removed from the cultivated circles of England, with the expressionless coast and the great sea perpetually foaming before him, he labored with a brotherly tenderness and a self-consuming zeal for the sailors. Like most men of genius he loved children ; he gathered a Sabbath-school of several hundred scholars, and he took especial pains in instructing and training a band of some seventy or eighty teachers for Sunday-school work·

Here he composed the sympathetic lyrics which are found in nearly all collections of church psalmody. Nearly all of these hymns, which are among the most perfect in the language, and which have spread over the Christian world, were written for his own church, a body composed in the main of seafaring people on a rude English coast.

His health was delicate, and the sword proved too sharp for the scabbard. In 1846, he found his strength failing and resolved to seek a reaction in travel. He had learned to love the poor, and his heart was wholly engrossed in his work among the sailors. He was prepared for death, but he yet wished to live. He felt, like Keats, that he had, as yet, accomplished nothing, that the influence that he had thus far been able to exert would quickly vanish from among mankind, and that his name would be " writ in water."

In a poem entitled, " Declining Days," he thus dis-
closes the secret of his pure, sympathetic heart:

> " Might verse of mine inspire
>   One virtuous aim, one high resolve impart;
> Light in one drooping soul a hallowed fire,
>   Or bind one broken heart,
>
> " Death would be sweeter then,
>   More calm my slumber 'neath the silent sod;
> Might I thus live to bless my fellow-men,
>   Or glorify my God."

In the same poem he makes the following prayer,
which was most remarkably answered:

> " Oh thou, whose touch can lend
>   Life to the dead, thy quickening grace supply;
> And grant me, swan-like, my last breath to spend
>   In song that may not die."

It was the autumn of 1847; the gloom of winter was
already settling upon the coast, and the pomps of decay
tinging the leaves. The pastor, who was now preparing
to leave the parish, and who seemed like one already
hovering over the verge of the grave, determined to
speak to his dear people once more, perhaps for the last
time. He dragged his attenuated form into the pulpit,
and delivered his parting discourse, while the great tears
rolled down the hardy faces of the worshippers. He
then administered the Lord's Supper to his spiritual children. Tired and exhausted, but with his heart still swelling with emotion, he went home. The old poetic inspiration came over him, and he wrote the words and music of
his last song. He had prayed that his last breath might
be spent " swan-like,"

" In songs that may not die."

and this effort was to prove a literal answer to his prayer·

The poem composed under these interesting circumstances was the following well-known hymn-chant:

> ABIDE with me: fast falls the eventide.
> The darkness deepens; Lord, with me abide:
> When other helpers fail, and comforts flee,
> Help of the helpless, O abide with me.
>
> Swift to its close ebbs out life's little day;
> Earth's joys grow dim, its glories pass away.
> Change and decay in all around I see;
> O Thou who changest not, abide with me.
>
> I need thy presence every passing hour;
> What but thy grace can foil the tempter's power?
> Who, like thyself, my guide and stay can be?
> Through cloud and sunshine, Lord, abide with me.
>
> I fear no foe, with thee at hand to bless:
> Ills have no weight, and tears no bitterness.
> Where is death's sting? where, grave, thy victory?
> I triumph still, if Thou abide with me.
>
> Hold Thou thy cross before my closing eyes;
> Shine through the gloom, and point me to the skies;
> Heaven's morning breaks, and earth's vain shadows flee!
> In life, in death, O Lord, abide with me.

He went to Nice. There at the foot of the Maritime Alps, in the climate of perpetual summer, with the mountain torrents singing around him, and the splendid Mediterranean before him, he passed the last days of his life. His death was that of a happy Christian poet. Like George Herbert and Charles Wesley, he sang while his strength lasted, and then quietly waited, till "rising from the sleep of death, he should join the hallelujahs of heaven.'

JOHN H. NEWMAN.

IN the year 1833, an English Episcopal clergyman Rev. John Henry Newman, was sailing over the Mediterranean, when suffering from the effects of a recent and an alarming illness. His religious feelings were agitated by the dissensions in the church at home, and an inward spiritual conflict was working a change in his views, until, w th perils at sea, sickness, doubt, and perplexity, he was made to feel that faith has but one reliance. In this state of mind, with a sky of Italian splendors and dangers above him, and the sea rocking the ship beneath, he composed one of the sweetest and most trustful of modern hymns :

> LEAD, Kindly Light, amid the encircling gloom,
> > Lead Thou me on ;
> The night is dark, and I am far from home,
> > Lead Thou me on.
> Keep Thou my feet ; I do not ask to see
> The distant scene ; one step enough for me.
>
> I was not ever thus, nor prayed that Thou
> > Shouldst lead me on ;
> I loved to choose and see my path ; but now
> > Lead Thou me on.
> I loved the garish day, and, spite of fears,
> Pride ruled my will : remember not past years.
>
> So long thy power hath blest me, sure it still
> > Will lead me on
> O'er moor and fen, o'er crag and torrent, till
> > The night is gone,
> And with the morn those angel faces smile
> Which I have loved long since, and lost awhile.

VIII. AUTOBIOGRAPHICAL HYMNS.

1. *DR. ISAAC WATTS: PERSONAL HYMNS AND HYMNS ON SPECIAL OCCASIONS.*
2. *CHARLES WESLEY: HYMNS FOR SPECIAL OCCASIONS.*
3. *JAMES MONTGOMERY· HYMNS OF PERSONAL EXPERIENCE.*
4. *THOMAS OLIVERS: "THE GOD OF ABRAM PRAISE."*
5. *MADAM GUYON'S HYMNS.*

AUTOBIOGRAPHICAL HYMNS.

DR. ISAAC WATTS:

PERSONAL HYMNS AND HYMNS ON SPECIAL OCCASIONS.

THE bicentennial of Dr. Watts has just been observed in England, and, among all the contributors to modern psalmody, no one has left a clearer and purer tone in the church. The calm, unsullied light of his fame is not dimmed; his name holds a steady place as a benefactor, and his best thoughts, like ministering angels, still traverse every portion of the Christian world on the multitudinous wings of song. His tomb in the unconsecrated dust in Bunhill Fields still invites the grateful steps of the traveller, and his effigy in Westminster Abbey commands a larger respect than the busts of kings. Few men's thoughts have so lived in the thoughts of others as have those of Dr. Watts.

The father of Dr. Watts was a deacon of the Independent church at Southampton. At the age of eighteen Isaac complained of the want of taste in the hymns then generally used, and was requested to produce something better. He accordingly wrote an original hymn for the close of a Sabbath service in Southampton. It was given out in the usual manner, by the clerk, and greatly pleased the worshippers. It was the hymn, beginning,

"Behold the glories of the Lamb."

He was invited to write other hymns for use in the same church, and soon produced a sufficient number to make a book. The book met a demand of the times, and was immediately popular.

Among his early hymns was one composed under very interesting circumstances. Dr. Watts was enamored of Miss Elizabeth Singer, afterwards the celebrated Mrs. Rowe, who was greatly admired for her personal beauty, intellectual graces, and moral excellences. Some of the most accomplished men of the time were among her friends, and several offered her their hands.

Dr. Watts proposed marriage to Miss Singer, and was rejected. He was small in stature and lacking in personal beauty. Miss Singer, in alluding to his intellectual worth, said that she "loved the jewel, but could not admire the casket that contained it." His disappointment was very great, and in the first shadow of it he thus exhibits the feelings of his heart:

> How vain are all things here below,
>   How false, and yet how fair!
> Each pleasure hath its poison too,
>   And every sweet a snare.
>
> The brightest things below the sky
>   Give but a flattering light;
> We should suspect some danger nigh
>   Where we possess delight.
>
> Our dearest joys and nearest friends,
>   The partners of our blood,
> How they divide our wavering minds,
>   And leave but half for God.

> The fondness of a creature's love,
>   How strong it strikes the sense;
> Thither the warm affections move,
>   Nor can we call them thence.
>
> My Saviour, let thy beauties be
>   My soul's eternal food:
> And grace command my heart away
>   From all created good.

The hymn, beginning,

> "There is a land of pure delight,"

associates itself with the natural scenery of Southampton, his native town. It was written while he was sitting at the window of a parlor, overlooking the river Itchen, and in full view of the Isle of Wight. The landscape there is very beautiful, and forms a model for a poet to employ in describing allegorically the passage of the soul from earth to the paradise above.

Watts lived a tranquil, uneventful life, passing thirty-four years in the seclusion of Alney Park, a nobleman's seat, where he had been invited to make a home. His health was always delicate. He both preached and wrote, but his best efforts were given to his pen.

A critical writer in the "Oxford Essays" fixes upon the hymn beginning,

> "When I survey the wondrous cross,'

as Dr. Watts' best original effort; and pronounces the rendering of the ninetieth Psalm, beginning,

> "Our God, our help in ages past,"

as his finest paraphrase. The latter indeed not only preserves the sublime and lofty spirit, but the grand and

shadowy imagery of the Hebrew lawgiver's poetical con-
templation :

> " A thousand ages in thy sight,
>   Are like an evening gone ;
> Short as the watch that ends the night,
>   Before the rising sun.

> " Time, like an ever-rolling stream,
>   Bears all its sons away ;
> They fly, forgotten, as a dream
>   Dies at the opening day.

> " The busy tribes of flesh and blood,
>   With all their cares and fears,
> Are carried downward by the flood,
>   And lost in following years."

Probably none of Dr. Watts' hymns has been so
widely used, and has held so steadily its character as the
interpreter of a common religious experience, as that beginning,

> " When I can read my title clear,
>   To mansions in the skies."

The last stanza of this hymn, beginning,

> " There I shall bathe my weary soul
>   In seas of heavenly rest,"

is supposed to have borrowed its pleasing imagery from
the scenery of the calm harbor of Southampton, in view
of which it was written. Cowper seems to have taken
his picture of the pious peasant woman's contentment
and hope, in the famous allusion to Voltaire in the poem
" Hope," from one of these stanzas. He speaks of the
humble cottager as one who

> " Just knows and knows no more, her Bible true,
> A truth the brilliant Frenchman never knew,
> And in that charter reads with sparkling eyes
> Her title to a treasure in the skies."

The hymn, beginning,

> "Jesus shall reign where'er the sun,"

which is in part a paraphrase of Psalm 72, is probably Watts' best ascription of praise, and his nearest approach to Bishop Ken's universal doxology. After five generations of service, it now seems to have entered an almost new field as a foreign missionary hymn.

Many of Watts' hymns were composed to be sung after special sermons, and were intended to combine the best thoughts of the subject on which the preacher had dwelt. Thus the hymn, beginning,

> " What shall a dying sinner do?"

was first sung after one of Dr. Watts' sermons from the text, Rom. 1 : 16, and was originally entitled, " The Gospel—the Power of God to Salvation." The hymn beginning,

> "And is this life prolonged to me?"

was written to follow a sermon on " The Right Improvement of Life," 1 Cor. 3 : 22. The hymn beginning,

> " How vast a treasure we possess,"

was written for a sermon on " The Christian Treasure," from the text, " All things are yours."

Many pleasing anecdotes are associated with certain of Watts' hymns, as with certain of John and Charles Wesley's. The hymn, " Not all the blood of beasts," was found by an intelligent Jewess on a wrapper of some parcel she had received from a store, and made such an impression upon her mind that she was led to a perusal of the Bible, and to become a Christian. On announcing the change in her views, she was abandoned by her husband, and thereafter lived a life of great destitution, but consoled by a satisfying and comforting faith. Dr. Belcher gives an anecdote of a young man who found his heart hardened by a severe sermon on the punishments of sin, but who was asked to read the hymn, beginning,

> "Show pity, Lord; O Lord, forgive."

The hymn produced a total change in his feelings, and he left the room in tears, and soon after was made the partaker of a rich religious experience. Watt's hymn beginning,

> "I 'll praise my Maker while I 've breath,"

was sung by John Wesley when dying.

Perhaps no hymn conveys a richer and riper religious experience, that accords with the best Christian sentiment, than that beginning,

> "My God, the spring of all my joys."

No stanza certainly was ever so often repeated in life's extremity, as the following:

> "Jesus can make a dying bed
> Feel soft as downy pillows are,
> While on his breast I lean my head,
> And breathe my life out sweetly there."

The serene close of Dr. Watts' life was in harmony with the consolations of this stanza. "I thank God," he used to say in old age, "that I can lie down with comfort at night, not being solicitous whether I awake in this world or another." He spoke of his physical sufferings as enabling him to "bear the will of God when he could no longer do it." He requested that these words only, *In uno Jesu omnia*, should follow the name and dates on his tomb.

CHARLES WESLEY:

HYMNS FOR SPECIAL OCCASIONS.

CHARLES WESLEY's hymns were written under a great variety of interesting circumstances, and nearly all furnish a record of personal experience. Thus his mellifluous hymn, beginning,

> "Oh, for a thousand tongues to sing,"

was written for the anniversary-day of one's conversion, probably just a year after his own conversion, thus being a retrospection. "Head of the church triumphant," was written during the war between England and France and Spain, and has reference to the Wesleyan persecutions in those troubled times. The hymn beginning,

> "Glory to God, whose sovereign grace,"

has reference to the wonderful revival among the Kingswood colliers, as do the hymns beginning,

> "Let all men rejoice, by Jesus restored,"

and

> "Brethren beloved, your calling see."

The hymns, beginning,

> " God of my life, to thee,"
> " Fountain of life, and all my joy,"

and

> " Away with our fears, the glad morning appears,"

were written on birthdays, and record the progress of spiritual attainment and experience.

> " Come, O thou all-victorious Lord,
>   Thy power to us make known ;
>   Strike with the hammer of thy word,
>   And break these hearts of stone,"

was composed in June, 1746, before preaching in the Isle of Portland, Dorsetshire, where the people were mostly employed in stone quarries.

" See how great a flame inspires," was written at the time of the author's wonderful success in preaching among the Newcastle colliers. The imagery recalls the large fires that burned in Newcastle by night. " Blow ye the trumpet, blow," first appeared in a tract entitled, " Hymns for the New Year," or Hymns for New Year's Day, 1755.

The hymn, beginning,

> " Forth in thy name, O Lord, I go,
>   My daily labors to pursue ;
>   Thee, only thee, resolved to know,
>   In all I think, or speak, or do,"

has reference to his itinerant preaching :

That, which is made to begin in many hymn-books with the second stanza,

> " Lo ! on a narrow neck of land,"

is said to have been written at Land's End in Cornwall,
with the British Channel and the broad Atlantic in view,
and surging around the " narrow neck of land " on either
hand:

> Lo ! on a narrow neck of land,
> 'Twixt two unbounded seas, I stand,
>   Secure, insensible :
> A point of time, a moment's space,
> Removes me to that heavenly place,
>   Or shuts me up in hell.
>
> O God, mine inmost soul convert,
> And deeply on my thoughtful heart
>   Eternal things impress :
> Give me to feel their solemn weight,
> And tremble on the brink of fate,
>   And wake to righteousness.

JAMES MONTGOMERY'S HYMNS OF RELIGIOUS EXPERIENCE.

On the fourth of November, 1871, it was just one
hundred years since James Montgomery was born in the
lowly home of a humble Moravian minister in Irvine, a
seaport town in Ayrshire, Scotland.   The lessons of hope
and faith in God which his parents early endeavored to
inculcate, made a deep impression upon his mind.

At the age of six, his parents placed him at a Moravian school at Fulneck, near Leeds, in Yorkshire, England.
Here he was kindly treated ; the discipline of the school,
so happily blending pleasant recreation with study, was
well calculated to inspire a love for study in the childish
mind ; while over all was thrown the sweet and holy in-

fluence of the religion of Jesus, whom they were taught to regard as a Brother and Friend, and whose kind protection and constant care they daily recognized and acknowledged. As he grew up, the world with its flattering voice proffered its delusive pleasures, and like too many others, Montgomery listened to its seductive call, and left the peaceful haven at Fulneck, to plunge into the toils and struggles of the outside world, a step he ever regretted. In "after years," he thus speaks of the event:

> A STAR from heaven once went astray,
>   A planet beautiful and bright;
> Which to the sun's diviner ray
>   Owed all its beauty and its light;
> Yet deemed, when self-sufficient grown,
> Its borrowed glory all its own.
>
> A secret impulse urged its course;
>   As, by a demon power possessed,
> With rash, unheeding, headlong force,
>   It wildly wandered seeking rest;
> Till, far beyond the solar range,
> It underwent a fearful change.
>
> Dim, as it went, its lustre grew,
>   Till utter darkness wrapt it round,
> And slow and slower as it flew,
>   Failure of warmth and strength it found;
> Congealed into a globe of ice,
> It seemed cast out of Paradise.

The cares of the world proved harassing, and its pleasures wholly unsatisfactory. His early religious instruction prevented him from mingling with the dissipated and the gay, and thus saved him from a course of sinful indulgence. Although his associations were morally pure, still as he had once known the love of God, he could not help contrasting the peace he then enjoyed with the feelings of unrest and gloom which now filled his mind.

Writing to a friend at this time, he thus describes the state of his feelings : "Such has been my education, such, I will venture to say, has been my experience in the morning of life, that I can never, never entirely reject it, and embrace any system of morality not grounded upon that revelation. What can I do ? I am tossed to and fro on a sea of doubts and perplexities ; the farther I am carried from that shore where I was once happily moored, the weaker grow my hopes of ever reaching another where I may anchor in safety : at the same time, my hopes of returning to the harbor I have left are diminished in proportion. This is the present state of my mind !" For a long time Montgomery's mind was a prey to despairing thoughts which led him to prayer, and at length the true light began to dawn ; a faint, feeble, flickering ray it was at first, but gradually grew stronger and brighter, until his heart was filled with the joy and peace of a bright hope in Christ. On his forty-third birthday he wrote to the presiding minister at Fulneck, asking to be readmitted into the Moravian congregation there ; a request which was most cordially granted.

His feelings upon the occasion are touchingly described in the following hymn :

PEOPLE of the living God
I have sought the world around,
Paths of sin and sorrow trod,
Peace and comfort nowhere found :

20

> Now to you my spirit turns—
>   Turns a fugitive unblest;
> Brethren, where your altar burns,
>   Oh, receive me into rest.
>
> Lonely I no longer roam,
>   Like the cloud, the wind, the wave;
> Where you dwell shall be my home,
>   Where you die shall be my grave.
> Mine the God whom you adore,
>   Your Redeemer shall be mine;
> Earth can fill my heart no more,
>   Every idol I resign.

From this time until the close of his life, Montgomery was actively employed in trying to do good, finding in the service of God that peace and happiness which the world failed to confer.

His hymns but reflect his own luminous experiences, and the experiences of the church, in all of whose joys, triumphs and sorrows he sympathized. His experience with the world had taught him that the soul has no rest but in God, and religion continually showed him that this rest was sweet and abiding:

> OH where shall rest be found,
>   Rest for the weary soul?
> 'T were vain the ocean's depths to sound
>   Or pierce to either pole.
>
> The world can never give
>   The bliss for which we sigh
> 'T is not the whole of life to live,
>   Nor all of death to die.

Beyond this vale of tears
  There is a life above, '
Unmeasured by the flight of years;
  And all that life is love.

There is a death, whose pang
  Outlasts the fleeting breath :
Oh what eternal horrors hang
  Around the second death !

Thou God of truth and grace !
  Teach us that death to shun ;
Lest we be banished from thy face,
  For evermore undone.

Solemn and grand is another view that he takes of his fading years

        " To see
All nature die, and find myself at ease,
In youth that seemed an immortality ;
But I am changed now, and feel with trees
A brotherhood, and in their obsequies
Think of my own."

In this mellow autumn time of life, with golden sheaves bending before him, he was called upon to produce a strain more noble than that which celebrates the deeds of warriors or the triumphs of conquerors.

  · At the annual meeting of the Church Missionary Society, in the spring of 1848, it was voted to hold a jubilee during the following autumn, in all of its departments throughout the world. Montgomery was invited to compose a jubilee hymn, which should be translated into other tongues, and sung in all lands on the festival day, and which should follow the circuit of the sun, and surround the earth with its melody. In a moment of poetic inspiration he seized his pen, and touched upon the majestic strain beginning, " The King of Glory we proclaim !"

The pleasant autumn came, and the venerable poet was permitted to join in singing the jubilant melody.

What an hour of triumph was that when the silver-haired man caught up the anthem that was encircling the lands ; when, after long watching and praying for the spread of the gospel of peace, he joined in a refrain of devout thanksgiving that came floating from the Celestial empire, from India, Smyrna, Syria, and the Nile, and that was borne onward to the tropic islands and the lands of the setting sun. That jubilant morning the missionaries of China sung, " The King of Glory we proclaim !" The converts of India, " The King of Glory we proclaim !" The dwellers by the shadows of the pyramids, " The King of Glory we proclaim !" Syria, made holy by the footsteps of the Redeemer, " The King of Glory we proclaim !" Christian Europe, like the voice of many waters, " The King of Glory we proclaim !" The tropic islands, in mellifluous notes and melting cadences, " The King of Glory we proclaim !" The simple fanes of the Western World, in voices ringing and clear, " The King of Glory we proclaim !" Thus from the going forth of the sun from the end of the heaven, and his circuit unto the ends of it, the great anthem rolled on from land to land, from sea to sea : " The King of Glory we proclaim !"

But when age had well battered his decaying tabernacle, he sung a sweeter strain than this. It indicates

how dear to his soul had become those spiritual mysteries
of which apostles wrote and prophets sung.

FOR ever with the Lord :
  Amen, so let it be :
Life from the dead is in that word,
  ' Tis immortality.

Here in the body pent,
  Absent from him I roam,
Yet nightly pitch my moving tent
  A day's march nearer home.

My Father's house on high—
  Home of my soul—how near
At times, to Faith's foreseeing eye,
  The golden gates appear.

Ah ! then my spirit faints
  To reach the land I love,
The bright inheritance of saints,
  Jerusalem above.

Yet clouds still intervene,
  And all my comfort flies ;
Like Noah's dove I flit between
  Rough seas and stormy skies.

Anon the clouds depart,
  The winds and waters cease,
And brightly o'er my gladdened heart
  Expands the bow of peace.

Beneath the glowing arch,
  Along the hallowed ground,
I see cherubic armies march,
  A camp of fire around.

20*

> I hear at morn and even,
>   At noon and midnight hour,
> The choral harmonies of heaven
>   Earth's Babel tongues o'erpower.
>
> Then, then I feel that He,
>   Remembered or forgot,
> The Lord is never far from me,
>   Though I perceive him not.

THOMAS OLIVERS.

" He was the worst boy that had been known in all that country for thirty years," wrote one of Thomas Olivers, a poor, fatherless boy, who in the friendlessness of youth had been led astray, and whose life had become continual dishonor.

But this youth had a tender conscience, which burned within him like a flame in his lonely hours, and, in all of his lapses and far-wanderings, he was ever resolving to amend his ways and to lead a life that would restore to him a calm mind.

At last these resolutions got the better of his moral weakness. He began to pray. At one time he prayed so often that his knees were made stiff by kneeling. But he was still weak, and was often led astray by profligate companions, and fell into open crime.

Conscience at length asserted its authority. He was completely broken down by an overwhelming sense of guilt. He felt now that there was no power within himself to save himself from evil, and that he must rely wholly upon Jesus as his Saviour, and the helpfulness of Divine providence and grace for salvation.

His prayers were now answered. Providence led him to an old seaport town in England, where Whitefield had an appointment to preach. He determined to go and hear the discourse of the great preacher, which promised to be helpful in a case like his.

"When the sermon began," he says, "I was one of the most abandoned and profligate young men living; before it ended I was a new creature." He was enabled at once to cast himself on the mercy of his Saviour, and felt at once uplifted and sustained by a strong arm—an experience that filled him with devout thankfulness to his dying day.

"The worst boy in all that country" was now a happy man. Besetting sins lost their attractions; heavenly joys were his continually. His faith was triumphant and majestic. "I saw God in everything," he said; "the heavens and the earth, and all therein, showed me something of Him."

He became a preacher. He was ready to endure any hardship, any persecution, anything for the strong love of Christ. In an hour of gratitude for so great a deliverance, and for such mighty power to uphold his soul, he thus penned his experience, which has become one of the thanksgivings of the ages:

> I. THE God of Abram praise,
>   Who reigns enthroned above:
>   Ancient of everlasting days,
>   And God of love:

JEHOVAH, GREAT I AM!
  By earth and heaven confessed,
I bow and bless the sacred Name,
  For ever blest.

The God of Abram praise,
  At whose supreme command
From earth I rise, and seek the joys
  At his right hand;
I all on earth forsake,
  Its wisdom, fame and power;
And him my only portion make,
  My shield and tower.

The God of Abram praise,
  Whose all-sufficient grace
Shall guide me all my happy days
  In all his ways :
He calls a worm his friend :
  He calls himself my God !
And he shall save me to the end,
  Through Jesus' blood.

He by himself hath sworn :
  I on his oath depend ;
I shall, on eagles' wings upborne,
  To heaven ascend ;
I shall behold his face ;
  I shall his power adore,
And sing the wonders of his grace
  For evermore.

II. THOUGH nature's strength decay,
    And earth and hell withstand.
  To Canaan's bounds I urge my way,
    At His command :

The watery deep I pass,
　With Jesus in my view;
And through the howling wilderness
　My way pursue.

The goodly land I see,
　With peace and plenty blest;
A land of sacred liberty
　And endless rest.
There milk and honey flow,
　And oil and wine abound;
And trees of life for ever grow,
　With mercy crowned.

There dwells the Lord our King,
　The Lord our Righteousness,
Triumphant o'er the world and sin,
　The Prince of Peace:
On Zion's sacred height,
　His kingdom still maintains;
And, glorious, with his saints in light
　For ever reigns.

HYMNS OF MADAME GUYON.

THE hymns of Madame Guyon, which are to be found
in Cowper's complete works, among his translations, or
which have been translated in part by Dr. Thomas Up-
ham, and a few of which are found in the hymn-books,
deserve to be better known and understood.　They are
the flowers and fruits of a very unusual and interesting
religious experience.

Madame Jeanne de la Motte Guyon was born at
Montargis, in 1648, and was educated, according to the

custom of the time, in the convents of her native city. She became pious in girlhood, and early consecrated her life to God.

The period in which she lived was particularly unfavorable for religious development—the dazzling but corrupt reign of Louis XIV. The people were taught to rely upon the observance of imposing rites and ceremonies for salvation, rather than upon a state of spiritual renovation and an inward acquaintance with God. But Mademoiselle de la Mothe found this sensational religion unsatisfying, and was anxious to know the truth and to practise it; and the Infinite Mind recognized and fulfilled the desire.

There was a devout father of the religious order of St. Francis, who had spent some five years in acts of devotion, for the purpose of seeking an experimental union with God, and of renouncing selfish interests and desires, that he might be better prepared to teach the truth in simplicity and purity, and God seems to have revealed himself to his spiritual perceptions, and to have granted him great spiritual peace, and delightful communion with the unseen world. Although a Romanist, he appears to have been truly converted. This devout father was impressed that it was his duty to labor for the conversion of some person of distinction; and, led by the inward monitor, he made a journey, and came to the house of M. de la Mothe, the father of Madame Guyon. He here became acquainted with the young inquirer. She related to him her religious exercises and inward conflicts, and appealed to him for counsel. The pious Franciscan, after listening to her narrative, was for a time silent, engaged in inward meditation and prayer. At length he said, " Your efforts have been unsuccessful, madame, because you have sought without what you can only find within. Seek God in your heart, and you will not fail to find him." A new light immediately broke upon Madame Guyon's mind; and the way of a spiritual acquaintance with God was clearly revealed.

She gives in her autobiography the following account of the spiritual exaltation and rapture that followed this great change:

" Nothing was more easy to me now than the practice of prayer. Hours passed away like moments, while I could hardly do anything else but pray. It was prayers of rejoicing and possession, wherein the taste of God was so great, so pure, so unblemished and uninterrupted, that it drew and absorbed the powers of my soul into a state of confiding and affectionate rest in God, existing without intellectual effort. I had now no sight but of Jesus Christ alone."

Madame Guyon at this period was about twenty years of age. She lived in the enjoyment of religion for many years, and, after the death of her husband, felt it her duty to become a spiritual instructor. She visited Grex, Thonon, and Glenoble, explaining the doctrine of clear religious experience, and engaging in works of benevolence. At this period she wrote a book, entitled, " Spiritual Torrents," in which religion is likened to a mountain stream ; and another, entitled, " A Short and Easy Method of Prayer," resembling in sentiment the mystical teachings of Molinos. In 1686, she went to Paris, where, with the Duchess of Beauvilliers, the Duchess of Bethune, the Countess of Guiche, and other ladies of rank, she organized meetings for religious conference and prayer. Her written works exerting a powerful influence, which was deemed adverse to the tenets of Rome, she was arrested by a royal order, and confined in the convent of St. Marie. She was released through the influence of Madame de Maintenon. Her opinions proving attractive to Madame de Maintenon, she was permitted to disseminate them in the seminary of St. Cyr. She became intimately acquainted with the learned and illustrious Fenelon, Archbishop of Cambrai, who favored her views in respect to inward holiness and a state of continuous fellowship with God. She was arrested on a false charge, and was imprisoned in the ancient castle of Vincennes. She was removed in 1689 to a prison in the Bastile. The walls of the fortress were nine feet thick, and a narrow slit through this massive masonry admitted all the light that ever reached the prisoner. The cells were narrow and dirty, and were covered with the mould of ages. They were damp and bitter cold in winter, and almost suffocating during the heat of summer. The prisoner was allowed no privileges, no books, no recreation, no employments.

> " Oh ! who can tell what days, what nights she spent
> Of tideless, waveless, sailless, shoreless woe !"

In this abode of sorrow Madame Guyon was for four years immured. Her cell was next to that of the Man of the Iron Mask. When she entered these gloomy portals, she expected to emerge only to suffer a martyr's death. In her former persecutions and imprisonments her triumphant spirit had never quailed. Her mind had been stayed on God, and kept in perfect peace. At times it seemed rapt up to heaven, and to dwell in an atmosphere of celestial light and glory. The radiance of the unseen world had dissipated the darkness of her dungeon. When imprisoned in the castle of Vincennes, her elevation of soul was such that she declared the very stones of her cell looked to her like rubies. How did she meet this last terrible ordeal, the worst that human power could devise? Listen:

"I feel no anxiety in view of what my enemies will do to me. I have no fear of anything but of being left to myself. So long as God is with me, neither imprisonment nor death will have any terrors. If they should proceed to extremities, and should put me to death, come and see me die. Do as Mary Magdalen did, who never left him that taught her the knowledge of pure love."

She was finally banished to Diziers, and died at the city of Blois, at a very advanced age.

Madame Guyon in her last years seemed to dwell, as it were, in Immanuel's land. She feared neither bastiles nor death. She speaks of her mind as fixed upon God alone, and enjoying uninterrupted communion with him.

Her poems are a revelation of her religious life and luminous experiences. She was accustomed to make all special trials and refreshments the subject of poetic composition. Perhaps no other writer has so fully embodied a long religious experience in verse.

Of her habitual resignation to the will of God, she says :

> " To me remains nor place nor time:
>   My country is in every clime ;
>   I can be calm and free from care
>   On any shore, since God is there.
>
> " While place we seek or place we shun,
>   The soul finds happiness in none ;
>   But, with a God to guide our way,
>   'T is equal joy to go or stay.
>
> " My country, Lord, art thou alone,
>   No other can I claim my own ;
>   The point where all my wishes meet,
>   My law, my love, life's only sweet.
>
> " Ah, then ! to his embrace repair,
>   My soul, thou art no stranger there,
>   There love divine shall be thy guard,
>   And peace and safety thy reward."

Again :

> " To me 't is equal, whether love ordain
>   My life or death, appoint me pain or ease;
>   My soul perceives no real ill in pain ;
>   In ease or health no real good she sees.
>
> " One good she covets, and that good alone:
>   To choose thy will from selfish bias free:
>   And to prefer a cottage to a throne,
>   And grief to comfort, if it pleases thee.
>
> " That we should bear the cross is thy command,
>   Die to the world, and live to self no more;
>   Suffer, unmoved, beneath the rudest hand ;
>   When shipwrecked pleased as when upon the shore."

Of her imprisonments:

> " Nor castle walls, nor dungeons deep,
>   Exclude His quickening beams,
>   There I can sit and sing and weep,
>   And dwell on heavenly themes.

> " There sorrow, for His sake, is found
>   A joy beyond compare,
>   There no presumptuous thoughts abound,
>   No pride can enter there."

Of her elevation of soul :

> " Oh, glory in which I am lost,
>   Too deep for the plummet of thought,
>   On an ocean of Deity tossed,
>   I am swallowed, I sink into naught,
>   Yet, lost and absorbed as I seem,
>   I chant to the praise of my King,
>   And, though overwhelmed by the theme
>   Am happy whenever I sing."

Madame Guyon loved to frequent solitary places for religious meditation, and to pray in solitude. Once when stopping near the banks of the Seine, she says: "On the banks of the river, finding a solitary place, I sought intercourse with my God. The communications of Divine love were unutterably sweet to my soul, in that retirement." She often alludes to her devotions in secluded places in her poems :

> " Here sweetly forgetting, and wholly forgot,
>   By the world and its turbulent throng,
>   The birds and the streams lend me many a note
>   That aids meditation and song.

> " Ah ! send me not back to the race of mankind,
>   Perversely by folly beguiled,
>   For where, in the crowds I have left, shall I find
>   The spirit and heart of a child ?
>
> " Here let me, though fixed in a desert, be free ;
>   A little one whom they despise,
>   Though lost to the world, if in union with thee,
>   Shall be holy and happy and wise."

Madame Guyon was accustomed, at one period of her life, to arise before daybreak for prayer :

> " Through the dark and silent night
>   On thy radiant smiles I dwelt,
>   And to see the dawning light
>   Was the keenest pain I felt."

She sings the spiritual happiness she found in communion with God, during the night season, in several noble poems, from which we add the following :

> " Night ! how I love thy silent shades,
>   My spirits they compose ;
>   The bliss of heaven my soul pervades,
>   In spite of all my woes.
>
> " Sleep at last has fled these eyes,
>   Nor do I regret his flight,
>   More alert my spirits rise,
>   And my heart is free and light.
>
> " Nature silent all around,
>   Not a single witness near ;
>   God as soon as sought is found,
>   And the flame of love burns clear."

IX. FAMILIAR HYMNS:

THEIR AUTHORS, DATES, ETC.,

AND PAGES OF THIS WORK WHERE ANY ARE MENTIONED.

ABIDE with me; fast falls the eventide. Lyte, 1847. See page 211.

A charge to keep I have. Charles Wesley, 1762.

A debtor to mercy alone. Augustus Montague Toplady. See page 29.

A few more years shall roll. Horatius Bonar, 1856. "Hymns of Faith and Hope."

A glory gilds the sacred page. Wm. Cowper, 1779. "Olney Hymns."

Ah, not like erring man is God. Henry Ustick Onderdonk, 1826.

All glory, laud, and honor. Theodulph; translated by J. M. Neale.
Written during imprisonment. Being sung by its author at his prison window in the hearing of the Emperor, Louis I., it gained the monk a pardon.

All hail the power of Jesus' name. Edward Perronet. See page 13.

All people that on earth do dwell. William Kethe.
Kethe was a clergyman, an army chaplain, and an exile with Knox at Geneva in 1555.

All praise to Thee, my God, this night. Thomas Ken. See page 17.

Almost persuaded now to believe. P. P. Bliss.
This is one of the revival hymns used by Ira D. Sankey, the coadjutor of Mr. Moody.

Am I a soldier of the Cross? Isaac Watts. 1709.

A Mountain Fastness is our God. Martin Luther; translated by W. R. Whittingham. See page 15.

And is this life prolonged to me? Watts. See page 223.

Angels from the realms of glory. James Montgomery, 1819.

Angels, roll the rock away. Thomas Scott and Thomas Gibbons, 1773.

Another six days' work is done.   Joseph Stennett.

A poor wayfaring man of grief.   James Montgomery.

Arm of the Lord, awake, awake!   William Shrubsole.

Around the throne of God in heaven.   Anne Houlditch Shepard.

Art thou weary, art thou languid!   Stephen the Sabaite; translated by
    J. M. Neale.
> Passed fifty-nine years in religious seclusion.   Stephen was born, 725; died, 794.

Asleep in Jesus, blessed sleep.   Margaret Mackay, 1832.
> Mrs. Mackay was a Scotch religious writer.

A star from heaven once went astray.   Jas. Montgomery.   See page 228.

As when the weary traveller gains.   John Newton.

Awake, and sing the song.   William Hammond, 1745.
> Mr. Hammond was a Calvinist Methodist, and a friend of Cennick.

Awake, my soul, and with the sun.   Thomas Ken.   See page 17.

Awake, my soul, stretch every nerve.   Philip Doddridge.

Awake, my soul, to joyful lays.   Samuel Medley, 1787.   See page 139.
> Rippon's Selection.   The following is the original:

> AWAKE, my soul, in joyful lays,
> And sing thy great Redeemer's praise;
> He justly claims a song from me,
> His loving-kindness is so free!
>
> He saw me ruined in the fall,
> Yet loved me, notwithstanding all;
> He saved me from my lost estate;
> His loving-kindness is so great.
>
> Through mighty hosts of cruel foes,
> Where earth and hell my way oppose,
> He safely leads my soul along;
> His loving-kindness is so strong!
>
> When earthly friends forsake me quite,
> And I have neither skill nor might,
> He's sure my helper to appear;
> His loving-kindness is so near!
>
> Often I feel my sinful heart
> Prone from my Jesus to depart;
> And though I oft have him forgot,
> His loving-kindness changes not.
>
> So when I pass death's gloomy vale
> And life and mortal powers shall fail,
> Oh may my last expiring breath
> His loving-kindness sing in death!

Awaked by Sinai's awful sound.   Written by Samson Occom in 1760.
> Occom was an Indian, and was converted in the revival of 1740, under Whitefield and
> his colaborers.   He preached among the Montauk Indians with great success; vis-
> ited England, where his preaching was attended by immense congregations, and
> where in a single year he preached nearly four hundred sermons.   His Indian school
> proved the beginning of Dartmouth College.

Away with our fears.   C. Wesley.   See page 226.

Before Jehovah's awful throne.   Isaac Watts.

Behold the glories of the Lamb.   Isaac Watts.   See page 219.

Behold the Saviour of mankind.   Samuel Wesley, 1719.

This hymn was saved from the flames at the burning of Epworth Parsonage, when John Wesley was a child.

Blest be the tie that binds.   John Fawcett.   See page 37.

Blow ye the trumpet, blow.   C. Wesley.   See page 226.

Bound upon th' accursed tree.   Milman.

Breast the wave, Christian.   Joseph Stammers, 1830.

Mr. Stammers is an English barrister.

Brethren beloved, your calling see.   C. Wesley.   See page 225.

Brief life is here our portion.   Bernard of Cluny; by J. M. Neale.

Brightly beams our Father's mercy.   P. P. Bliss.

Brightest and best of the sons of the morning.   Reginald Heber, 1811.

By cool Siloam's shady rill.   Reginald Heber, 1812.   See page 155.

Calm on the listening ear of night.   Edmund Hamilton Sears, 1837.

Originally appeared in the Boston *Observer*.

Children of the Heavenly King.   John Cennick, 1742.

The following beautiful stanza is usually altered or omitted:

"O ye banished seed, be glad !
Christ our Advocate is made ;
Us to save, our flesh assumes ;
Brother to our souls becomes."

Come, all ye saints, to Pisgah's mountain.   Rev. J. W. Dadmun.

This is a hymn of the heart.   Mr. Dadmun says, " I never wrote but one hymn that I consider worth naming; and that was written on the death of three of my children, all of whom died in the short space of three months.   The title of it is, ' Our Loved Ones in Heaven,' and it was composed in 1862.   It was the expression of my faith in God, and hope of a glorious immortality, when called to part with my ' loved ones.'   I published it in the ' New Melodeon,' pages 48–9."

The following is the first verse of the hymn:

" Come, all ye saints, to Pisgah's mountain, Some of bright crowns of glory are singing,
Come, view your home beyond the tide ; Some of dear ones who stand near the shore.
Hear now the voices of your loved ones, For the fond heart must ever be clinging
What they sing on the other side: To the faithful we love evermore."

Come, Holy Spirit, Heavenly Dove.   Isaac Watts, 1707.

Come, let us anew our journey pursue.   C. Wesley.   See page 109.

Come, let us join our cheerful songs.   Isaac Watts, 1709.

Come, let us join our friends above.   C. Wesley, 1759.   " Funeral Hymns."

Come, my soul, thy suit prepare.   John Newton.

Come, O thou all-victorious Lord. C. Wesley. See page 226.

Come, O thou Traveller unknown. C. Wesley.

Come, thou Almighty King. Charles Wesley.

Come, thou Fount of every blessing. Robinson. See page 42.

> Two original stanzas in this hymn are omitted in all modern collections. They are

> "Oh, that day when, freed from sinning,
>   I shall see thy lovely face;
> Robéd then in blood-washed linen,
>   Now I'll sing thy sovereign grace.
> Come, dear Lord, no longer tarry,
>   Take my raptured soul away;
> Send thine angels down to carry
>   Me to realms of endless day.

> " If thou ever didst discover
>   Unto me the promised land,
> Bid me now the stream pass over,
>   On the heavenly border stand.
> Help surmount whate'er opposes,
>   Unto thy embraces fly;
> Speak the word thou didst to Moses,
>   Bid me get me up and die."

Come, thou Holy Spirit, come. King Robert II. See page 67.

Come to Jesus. Anonymous.

> This refrain was very popular in Scotland some years ago, when multitudes used to sing it after listening to fervent preaching in the open air.

Come, we that love the Lord. Isaac Watts.

Come, ye disconsolate, where'er ye languish. Moore.

Come, ye sinners, poor and needy. Joseph Hart. See page 35.

Commit thou all thy grief's. Gerhardt. See page 82.

Daily, daily sing the praises. Gould. See page 154.

Day of Judgment, Day of wonders. John Newton.

Day of wrath ; oh, day of mourning. Thomas of Celano; translated by W. F. Irons, Dean Alford, and scores of others.

> The following is the Latin original:

> Dies iræ, dies illa.
> Solvet sæclum in favillâ,
> Teste David cum sibyllâ.

> Judex ergo cùm sedebit,
> Quidquid latet apparebit,
> Nil inultum remanebit.

> Quantus tremor est futurus,
> Quando judex est venturus,
> Cuncta stricte discussurus !

> Quid sum miser tunc dicturus
> Quem patronum rogaturus,
> Cum vix justus sit securus ?

> Tuba, mirum spargens sonum
> Per sepulchra regionum,
> Coget omnes ante thronum.

> Rex tremendæ majestatis,
> Qui salvandos salvas gratis,
> Salva me, fons pietatis.

> Mors stupebit, et natura,
> Cum resurget creatura
> Judicanti responsura.

> Recordare, Jesu pie,
> Quod sum causa tuæ viæ,
> Ne me perdas illâ die.

> Liber scriptus proferetur,
> In quo totem continetur
> Unde mundus judicetur.

> Quærens me sedisti lassus,
> Redemisti crucem passus;
> Tantus labor non sit cassus.

-Juste judex ultionis,
Donum fac remissionis
Ante diem rationis.

Ingemisco tanquam reus
Culpâ rubet vultus meus
Supplicanti parce, Deus !

Qui Mariam absolvisti,
Et latronem exaudisti,
Mihi quoque spem dedisti.

Preces meæ non sunt dignæ;
Sed tu, bonus, fac benigne,
Nec perenni cremer igne.

Inter oves locum præsta,
Et ab hœdis me sequestra,
Statuens in parte dextrâ.

Confutatis maledictis,
Flammis acribus addictis,
Voca me cum benedictis !

Oro supplex et acclinis,
Cor contritum quasi cinis;
Gere curam mei finis.

Lacrymosa dies illa,
Quâ resurget ex favillâ
Judicandus homo reus;
Huic ergo parce, Deus !

Pie Jesu, Domine, dona eis requiem.   Amen.

Dear as thou wert, and justly dear.   Thomas Dale, 1797.
     A funeral piece in Dale's " Widow of Nain."

Depth of mercy! can there be ?   C. Wesley.

Did Christ o'er sinners weep ?   Beddome, 1787.

Ein' feste Burg ist unser Gott.   Luther.   See page 15.

Ev'n such is time, that takes on trust.   Raleigh.   See page 80.

Fade, fade, each earthly joy.   Bonar.   See page 196.

Far from the world, O Lord, I flee.   Cowper.   See pages 44, 49.

Father, whate'er of earthly bliss.   Anne Steele, 1760.   See page 58.

Fear not, O little flock, the foe.   Altenburg.   See page 70.

Fierce was the wild billow.   Anatolius and J. M. Neale.   See page 173.

For ever with the Lord.   James Montgomery.   See page 233.

For thee, O dear, dear country.   Bernard of Cluny ; translated by J. M.
     Neale.

Forth in thy name, O Lord, I go.   C. Wesley.   See page 226.

Fountain of life and all my joy.   C. Wesley.   See page 226.

From all that dwell below the skies.   Isaac Watts, 1719.

From every stormy wind that blows.   Hugh Stowell.
     From Stowell's " Pleasures of Religion."

From Greenland's icy mountains.   Reginald Heber.   See page 40.

From out this dim and gloomy hollow.   Schiller.   See page 85.

Give me my scallop-shell of quiet.   Walter Raleigh.   See page 79.

Glorious things of thee are spoken.   John Newton, 1779.

Glory and thanks to God we give.   Written by Charles Wesley after a deliverance from death.

> "On his third visit to Leeds," says one describing the somewhat remarkable occasion "he met the society in an old upper room, which was dense'y packed, and crowds could not gain admission.   He removed nearer the door, that those without might hear him, and drew the people after him.   Instantly the rafters broke, and the floor sunk, and more than one hundred people fell into the room below."   Several were seriously injured, but none killed; and the new converts, instead of being overcome with fear, broke forth in utterances of triumphant faith.

Glory to God, whose sovereign grace.   C. Wesley.   See page 225.

Glory to thee, my God, this night.   Ken.   See page 22.

God bless our native land.   From the German, By C. T. Brooks and J. S. Dwight, 1844.

God calling yet—and shall I never hearken?   Tersteegen.   See page 164.

God is our refuge in distress.   Tate and Brady.

> Tate was poet-laureate from 1690 to 1715.   His "Metrical Version of the Psalms" was the standard and authorized version of the times.   He was assisted in the composition of this work by Nicholas Brady.

God of my life, to thee.   C. Wesley.   See page 226.

God moves in a mysterious way.   William Cowper.   See page 44.

Golden head so lowly bending.   Putnam's Magazine.   See page 148.

Go to dark Gethsemane.   James Montgomery, 1822.

Grace! 'tis a charming sound.   Philip Doddridge.

Great God, what do I see and hear !   William Bengo Collyer.

> Mr. Collyer was pastor of a Congregational church in London from 1811 to 1854.

Guide me, O thou Great Jehovah.   William Williams.   See page 30.

Hail, thou long-expected Jesus.   C. Wesley.   "Hymns for the Nativity," 1745.

Hail, thou once-despised Jesus.   John Bakewell.

> Wesley says that Bakewell "adorned the doctrine of God our Saviour 80 years, and preached His gospel 70 years.   He was a friend of Olivers, who wrote "The God of Abram praise" at his house.

Hail to the Lord's Anointed.   James Montgomery.

Hark! hark! my soul ; angelic songs are swelling.   F. W. Faber.   See page 188.

Hark! the glad sound! the Saviour comes.   Philip Doddridge.

> Written to supplement a sermon preached Dec. 28, 1755.

Hark! the voice of love and mercy.   Jonathan Evans.   See page 131.

Hark! what mean those holy voices?   John Cawood, 1775-1852.

Have you on the Lord believed?   P. P. Bliss.

Heaven is my home.   Taylor.   See page 159.

He leadeth me! oh, blessed thought.   Gilmore.   See page 167.

He sendeth sun, He sendeth shower.   S. F. Adams.   See page 205.

High the angel choirs are raising.   Kempis.   See page 77.

How are thy servants blest, O Lord.   Addison.   See page 98.

How beauteous are their feet.   Isaac Watts.

How firm a foundation, ye saints of the Lord.   George Keith, 1787.

How happy are the little flock.   C. Wesley.   See page 114.

How happy every child of grace.   C. Wesley.

How happy, gracious Lord, are we.   C. Wesley.   See page 108.

How happy is the pilgrim's lot.   John Wesley.   See page 104.

> This hymn, which is, perhaps, the most condensed and perfect narrative we have of
> John Wesley's religious experience, was written before his marriage, and the original
> contains the following stanza, omitted in all collections:

> "I have no sharer of my heart   Only betrothed to Christ am I,
>   To rob my Saviour of a part,   And wait his coming from the sky,
>   And desecrate the whole.   To wed my happy soul."

How sweetly flowed the Gospel sound.   Bowring.

> This popular church hymn appears in Sir John Bowring's "Matins and Vespers,"
> and was evidently inspired by true devotional feeling.   He says of the hymns in the
> collection in which it appeared:

> "So much of serene and so much of joyful feeling, so much of calm and grateful
> recollection, so much of present peace and comfort, and so much of holy and trans-
> porting hope, are connected with the cultivation of the devotional spirit, that to
> assist its exercises, to administer to its wants, and to accompany its heavenly aspi-
> rations, are objects worthy of the noblest, the best ambitions.

> "In attempting to give some of the ornaments of song to such contemplations,
> and such expressions as become those who have formed a true estimate of life, and
> of the ends of living, I trust I have never forgotten that the substance of piety is of
> higher interest than any of its decorations, that the presence of truth is of more im-
> portance than the garment it wears.

> "I have often witnessed, with complacency and delight, the consoling influence
> produced by the recollection of some passage of devotional poetry, under circum-
> stances the most disheartening and sufferings the most oppressive.   Should any
> fragment of this little book, remembered and dwelt upon in moments of gloom and
> anxiety, tend to restore peace, to awaken fortitude, to create, to renew, or to
> strengthen confidence in Heaven, I shall have obtained the boon for which I pray—
> the end to which I aspire.

> "These Hymns were not written in the pursuit of fame or literary triumph. They
> are full of borrowed images, of thoughts and feelings excited less by my own con-
> templations than by the writings of others."

How sweetly flowed the gospel sound   " Come, wanderers, to my Father's home ;
  From lips of gentleness and grace,   Come, all ye weary ones, and rest !"
When listening thousands gathered round,   Yes! sacred Teacher, we will come,
  And joy and reverence filled the place !   Obey thee, love thee, and be blest!

From heaven he came—of heaven he spoke,   Decay, then, tenements of dust !
  To heaven he led his followers' way ;   Pillars of earthly pride, decay !
Dark clouds of gloomy night he broke,   A nobler mansion waits the just,
  Unveiling an immortal day.   And Jesus has prepared the way.

     The solemn chant, " From the recesses of a lowly spirit," appears in the same volume.

How sweet the name of Jesus sounds.   John Newton.

How vain are all things here below.   Watts.   See page 220.

How vast a treasure we possess.   Watts.   See page 223.

I am so glad that our Father in heaven.   Bliss.   See page 169.

I am trusting Lord in Thee.   William McDonald.

     Mr. McDonald is a most successful revival preacher in the Methodist connection, and
     often makes use of this hymn in inviting the penitent to kneel for prayers.

I gave my life for thee.

     Written in youth by Miss Frances Ridley Havergal, daughter of Rev. W. H. Haver-
     gal.   See page 169.

I have entered the valley of blessing, so sweet.   Annie Wittenmeyer.

I heard the voice of Jesus say.   H. Bonar.   See page 194.

I hear thy welcome voice.   L. Hartsough.

I hear the Saviour say.   Mrs. E. M. Hall.

I lay my wants on Jesus.   Bonar.   See page 195.

I'll praise my Maker with my breath.   Isaac Watts.   See page 224.

I'm but a stranger here.   Taylor.   See page 160.

I love my God, but with no love of mine.   Madame Guyon.

I love thy kingdom, Lord.   Timothy Dwight.

     Timothy Dwight was born at Northampton, Mass., May 14, 1752, and graduated at
     Yale College at the age of thirteen.   He wrote several religious poems of considera-
     ble length.   In 1795 he was elected President of Yale College, and in 1800 he revised
     Watts' Psalms, at the request of the General Association of Connecticut, adding a
     number of translations of his own.   Among the best known of these original produc-
     tions is the above hymn.

I love thy kingdom, Lord,   I love thy Church, O God ;
  The house of thine abode,   Her walls before thee stand,
The Church our blest Redeemer saved   Dear as the apple of thine eye,
  With his own precious blood.   And graven on thy hand.

It e'er to bless thy sons
  My voice or hands deny,
These hands let useful skill forsake,
  This voice in silence die.

For her my tears shall fall;
  For her my prayers ascend;
To her my cares and toils be given,
  Till toils and cares shall end.

Beyond my highest joy
  I prize her heavenly ways,
Her sweet communion, solemn vows,
  Her hymns of love and praise.

Jesus, thou Friend divine,
  Our Saviour and our King,
Thy hand from every snare and foe
  Shall great deliverance bring.

Sure as thy truth shall last,
  To Sion shall be given
The brightest glories earth can yield,
  And brighter bliss of heaven.

I love Thee, I love Thee, etc. Jer. Ingalls, 1805.

I love to steal awhile away. See page 48.

This hymn, by Mrs. Phœbe H. Brown, originally began with a stanza, which is omitted in all collections:

Yes, when the toilsome day is gone.
  And night with banners gray
Steals silently the glade along,
  In sunlight's soft array.

In all my Lord's appointed ways.

Rev. John Ryland, D. D., an English Baptist minister, composed this hymn while listening to a sermon preached in his own pulpit. "Dr. Ryland." says an account, "sat in the desk below the pulpit to read the hymns; and, as his brother proceeded, every head of the discourse was turned into poetry, which at the end of the sermon was duly read, and a portion of it sung."

In de dark wood, no Indian nigh. Apes. See page 181.

In some way or other the Lord will provide.

Written by Mrs. M. A. W. Cook, wife of Rev. Parsons Cook of Massachusetts. It was written for the "American Messenger," and first published in 1870. It was set to music by Prof. C. S. Harrington, of the Wesleyan University at Middletown, Conn. The hymn is very popular both in America and Germany. We give both the English and the German versions.

In some way or other the Lord will pro-
     vide;
  It may not be my way,
  It may not be thy way,
  And yet, in his own way,
  "The Lord will provide."

At some time or other the Lord will pro-
     vide;
  It may not be my time,
  It may not be thy time,
  And yet, in his own time,
  "The Lord will provide."

Despond then no longer; the Lord will pro-
     vide;
  And this be the token—
  No word he hath spoken
  Was ever yet broken—
  "The Lord will provide."

March on, then, right boldly; the sea shall
     - divide;
  The pathway made glorious,
  With shoutings victorious
  We'll join in the chorus,
  "The Lord will provide."

DER HERR WIRD'S VERSEHEN.

Sei's so oder anders, der Herr wird's ver-
    sehen;
    Mag's nicht sein wie ich will,
    Mag's nicht sein wie du willst,
    Doch wird's sein wie Er will:
    Der Herr wird's versehen.

Sei's jetzt oder später, der Herr wird's ver-
    sehen;
    Mag's nicht sein wann ich will,
    Mag's nicht sein wann du willst,
    Doch wird's sein wann Er will:
    Der Herr wird's versehen.

So zage nicht langer, der Herr wird's versehen;
    Und dies sei dein Zeichen:
    Nie hat Er gebrochen
    Was einst Er gesprochen;
    Der Herr wird's versehen.

In the Christian's home in glory. Rev. J. Y. Harmer.

In the cross of Christ I glory. Bowring.

In the silent midnight watches. By Arthur Cleveland Coxe.

> Mr. Coxe was born in New Jersey, May 10, 1818, was educated at the General Theological Seminary, New York, and in 1840 published a volume of religious poems, which passed through five editions.

Is there a thing beneath the sun? Tersteegen. See page 162.

It came upon the midnight clear. Edmund Hamilton Sears, 1850.

I think, when I read that sweet story of old. Jemima Luke. See p. 146.

It is told me I must die. Langhorn. See page 117.

I want to be an angel. Mrs. Gill. See page 150.

I would not live alway, I ask not to stay.

> Written by Rev. Dr. William A. Muhlenberg. The following is the original hymn, as it appeared in the " Episcopal Recorder, Philadelphia, in 1824:

I would not live alway—live alway below!
Oh, no! I 'll not linger when bidden to go;
The days of our pilgrimage granted us here
Are enough for life's woes, full enough for
    its cheer;
Would I shrink from the paths which the
    prophets of God,
Apostles and martyrs so joyfully trod?
Like a spirit unblest o'er the earth wou'd I
    roam,
While brethren and friends are all hastening
    home?

I would not live alway; I ask not to stay
Where storm after storm rises dark o'er the
    way;
Where, seeking for rest, we but hover around,
Like the patriarch's bird, and no resting is
    found;

Where Hope, when she paints her gay bow
    in the air,
Leaves its brilliance to fade in the night of
    despair,
And joy's fleeting angel ne'er sheds a glad
    ray,
Save the gleam of the plumage that bears
    him away.

I would not live alway, thus fettered by
    sin,
Temptation without and corruption within;
In a moment of strength if I sever the chain,
Scarce the victory is mine ere I 'm captive
    again;
E'en the rapture of pardon is mingled with
    fears,
And the cup of thanksgiving with penitent
    tears;

The festival trump calls for jubilant songs,
But my spirit her own *miserere* prolongs.

I would not live alway! no, welcome the
  tomb;
Since Jesus hath lain there, I dread not its
  gloom;
Where He deigned to sleep I 'll too bow my
  head,
All peaceful to slumber on that hallowed bed.
Then the glorious daybreak to follow that
  night,
The orient gleam of the angels of light,
With their clarion call for the sleepers to
  rise
And chant forth their matins, away to the
  skies.

Who, who would live alway, away from his
  God,
Away from yon heaven, that blissful abode,

Where the rivers of pleasure flow o'er the
  bright plains,
And the noontide of glory eternally reigns;
Where the saints of all ages in harmony meet,
Their Saviour and brethren transported to
  greet,
While the songs of salvation exultingly roll,
And the smile of the Lord is the feast of the
  soul ?

That heavenly music ! what is it I hear ?
The notes of the harper ring sweet in mine
  ear !
And see, soft unfolding, those portals of gold,
The King, all arrayed in his beauty, behold!
Oh, give me, oh, give me the wings of a
  dove,
To adore Him, be near Him, enrapt with
  his love !
I but wait the summons, I list for the word:
Alleluia ! Amen ! evermore with the Lord!"

The following is an authorized account of the publication of the poem in the form of
a hymn:

"In 1826 the General Convention of the Episcopal Church appointed a committee to prepare a collection of hymns, to be added to the fifty-six, then the whole
number attached to the prayer-book. This measure was in consequence of an awakened interest in hymnology, brought about by articles on 'Church Poetry,' and 'A
Plea for Christian Hymns,' addressed to the authorities of the church by Dr. Muhlenberg through the religious press. He was chosen by the convention as one of
the committee, and the Rev. Dr. H. Onderdonk, the rector of St. Ann's, in Brook-
lyn, as another. The poem, 'I would not live alway,' Dr. Onderdonk abridged
into a hymn of suitable length for divine worship, and submitted to Dr. Muhlenberg
for revision. There were no changes from the sentiment of the original composition ; only four lines in the new differed from the original, and those in a few
words, as will be seen by comparison between the two."

Jerusalem, my happy home.   Anon.   See page 158.

Jerusalem, the golden.   Bernard of Cluny; translated by J. M. Neale.

From a manuscript of three thousand lines, entitled "De Contemptu Mundi.'

Jesus, and shall it ever be.   Joseph Grigg.   See page 60.

Jesus Christ is risen to-day.   Anon.

Jesus, I my cross have taken.   Henry Francis Lyte.   See page 211.

Jesus lives no longer now.   C. F. Gellert; translated by Francis Cox.

Jesus, lover of my soul.   See page 174.

Two stories are told of the origin of this hymn, though neither of them can now be
certified as trustworthy:
John and Charles Wesley, with Richard Pilmore, according to one account, were once

holding a twilight meeting, when being attacked with great fury by a mob, they found a refuge in a spring-house, where they were at last befriended by the darkness of night. Here they struck a light with a flint, quenched their thirst and bathed their hands and faces in the water that flowed by. Then Charles Wesley was moved to write down the feelings of the hour in a hymn. He made use of a bit of lead which he had hammered into a pencil. The hymn thus written was, " Jesus, Lover of my Soul."

Another account says, that Charles Wesley was one day sitting by an open window, when his attention was attracted by a little bird, pursued by a hawk. In its terror, the bird sped towards the window, and sought refuge in the poet's bosom. The thought came to Wesley that he had a refuge in the bosom of Christ when pursued by temptation and persecution; and, under the influence of the feeling excited by the incident, he wrote the hymn.

Jesus, meek and gentle. George Rundle Trynne, 1856.

Jesus, my all, to heaven is gone. John Cennick. See page 54.

Jesus, pro me perforatus. Gladstone. See page 28.

Jesus shall reign where'er the sun. Isaac Watts, 1719. See page 223.

Jesus, tender Shepherd, hear me. Mary L. Duncan, 1814–1841.
Written as an evening prayer for her own children.

Jesus, the very thought of Thee. Bernard ; translated by G. E. Caswell
Wesley calls Bernard of Clairvaux, "The best monk that ever lived."

Jesus, Thy blood and righteousness. Count Zinzendorf; translated by John Wesley. See page 99.

Joy to the world! the Lord is come. Isaac Watts.

Just as I am, without one plea. Charlotte Elliott. See page 155.

Knocking, knocking, ever knocking. Mrs. H. E. B. Stowe.
The original poem is somewhat different from the Sunday-school hymn. It was first published in the *Christian Watchman and Reflector.*

Knocking, knocking, ever knocking;
    Who is there ?
'Tis a Pilgrim, strange and kingly,
    Never such was seen before;
Ah, sweet soul, for such a Wonder,
    Undo the door.

" No, the door is hard to open,
Hinges rusty, latch is broken;
    Bid Him go.
Wherefore with that knocking dreary
Scare the sleep from one so weary ?
    Say him, No."

Knocking, knocking, ever knocking.
    What, still there ?
O sweet soul, but once behold Him,
    With the glory-crownéd hair.

And those eyes so strange and tender
    Waiting there:
Open, open, once behold Him—
    Him so fair.

"Oh, that door ! why wilt thou vex me,
Coming ever to perplex me ?
For the key is stiff and rusty,
And the bolt is clogged and dusty ;
Many-fingered ivy vine
Seals it fast with twist and twine ;
Weeds of years and years before
Choke the passage to that door.

" Knocking, knocking ! What, still knocking?
    He still there ?
What's the hour ? The night is waning,
In my heart a drear complaining.

And a sad unrest !
Ah, this knocking.   It disturbs me—
Scares my sleep with dreams unblest.
Rest—ah ! rest.

Rest, dear soul, he longs to give thee;
Thou hast only dreamed of pleasure—
Dreamed of gifts and golden treasure—
Dreamed of jewels in thy keeping,
Waked to weariness and weeping;
Open to thy soul's one Lover,
And thy night of dreams is over.
The true gifts He brings, have seeming
More than all thy faded dreaming.

Did she open ?   Doth she ?   Will she ?
So, as wondering we behold,
Grows the picture to a sign,
Pressed upon your soul and mine;
For, in every breast that liveth
Is that strange, mysterious door:
Though forsaken and betangled,
Folly-gnarled and weed-bejangled,
Dusty, rusty, and forgotten;
There the piercèd hand still knocketh,
And with ever-patient watching,
With the sad eyes true and tender,
With the glory-crownèd hair—
Still a God is waiting there.

Land ahead ! its fruits are waving.   See page 166.

Lead, kindly Light, amid the encircling gloom.   John Henry Newman.
See page 215.

"I was aching to get home; yet for want of a vessel, was kept at Palermo for three
weeks. At last I got off on an orange-boat bound for Marseilles. We were be-
calmed a whole week in the Straits of Bonifacio. There it was that I wrote the lines
'Lead, kindly Light,' which have become well known."   Newman.

Let all men rejoice, by Jesus restored.   C. Wesley.   See page 225.

Light of those whose dreary dwelling.   Charles Wesley, 1745.

'Listed in the cause of sin.   Charles Wesley.   See page 175.

Little travellers Zionward.   Edmeston.   See page 165.

Lo! He comes, with clouds descending.   C. Wesley and F. Cennick.

Lo! on a narrow neck of land.   C. Wesley.   See page 226.

Lord, dismiss us with thy blessing.   Walter Shirley.   See page 223.

Lord, how secure and blest are they.   Watts.

Lord, in the morning Thou shalt hear.   Isaac Watts, 1719.

Lord of the Sabbath, hear our vows.   Doddridge.   See page 34.

Love divine, all love excelling.   Charles Wesley, 1746.

Mercy, O thou Son of David.   Newton.

Mighty God, while angels bless thee.   Robinson.   See page 43.

Must Jesus bear the cross alone?

First appeared in the Plymouth Collection, 1855. Written by G. N. Allen.

My country, 't is of thee.

Written by Rev. S. F. Smith, D. D., in 1831-32, and first sung in public in Park street
church, Boston, on the occasion of a children's celebration of July 4, 1831 or 1832.

22*

Dr. Smith, a Baptist clergyman and editor, contributed twenty-six hymns to the Psalmist, and eight hymns to the American Sabbath Hymn-Book.

My eyes have seen the glory of the coming of the Lord.   Julia Ward Howe.

Written after a visit to the camps on the Potomac during the early part of the Union war, and published in the Atlantic Monthly.

My faith looks up to Thee.   Ray Palmer, 1833.   See page 209.

My God, my Father, while I stray.   Charlotte Elliott.   See page 200.

My God, I love Thee, not because.   St. Francis Xavier; translated by G. E. Caswell.   See page 71.

My God, permit me not to be.   Isaac Watts, 1709.

My God, the spring of all my joys.   Watts.   See page 224.

My gracious Redeemer I love.   Benjamin Francis.

Mr. Francis was a Baptist minister, (1734-1799).   He joined the church at the age of fifteen; he preached to a humble congregation, refusing a pastorate offered him in London.

My hope is built on nothing less.

By Edward Mote, an English Baptist minister; born, 1797.

My opening eyes with rapture see.   F. Hutton.

My Saviour, my Almighty Friend.   Watts.

My soul, be on thy guard.   George Heath, 1781.

Nearer, my God, to Thee.   Sarah Flower Adams.   See page 201.

No war nor battle sound.   Milton.

Written in his twenty-first year.   The original has thirty-one stanzas.

Now I lay me down to sleep.   See page 148.

"Now I lay"—repeat it, darling.   Lutheran Monthly.   See page 149.

Now is the accepted time.   John Dobell.

This and other hymns by the same author, were published at the suggestion of a pious lady in Cornwall, who was an invalid, and whom Dobell frequently visited in sickness.   She said to him, "I wish I could see before I die a hymn-book full of Christ and his gospel, without any mixture of human merit."   It became the aim of Dobell to compose and compile such a book.

O bliss of the purified. bliss of the free.   Rev. F. Bottome.

O Day of rest and gladness.   Christopher Wordsworth, 1862.

O Deus, ego amo Te.   Francis Zavier.   See page 71.

O'er the gloomy hills of darkness.   William Williams.   See page 31.

Oft in danger, oft in woe.   F. F. Maitland and H. K. White.

> The first ten lines of this hymn were left a fragment by Kirke White, written on the back of one of his mathematical papers.   They came, after his death. into the hands of Dr. Collyer, who published them, with six not very successful lines of his own added, in his Hymn-book of 1812, where the hymn is numbered 867.   The task of finishing it was more happily accomplished by Miss F. F. Maitland.

O God, our help in ages past.   Isaac Watts.

O happy day, that stays my choice.   Philip Doddridge.

O happy saints, who dwell in light.

> Written by Rev. John Berridge.   His epitaph, composed by himself, is a brief memoir:
> " Here lie the earthly remains of John Berridge, late vicar of Everton, and an itinerant servant of Jesus Christ, who loved his Master and His work, and after running His errands many years, was called up to wait on Him above.
> " Reader, art thou born again ?
> " No salvation without the new birth.
> " I was born in sin, February, 1716.
> " Remained ignorant of my fallen state till 1730.
> " Lived proudly on faith and works for salvation till 1751.
> " Admitted to Everton vicarage, 1755.
> " Fled to Jesus alone for refuge, 1756.
> " Fell asleep in Jesus Christ, —"   (1793.)

Oh come, all ye faithful.   Translated by Frederic Oakeley.   Mediæval.

Oh come, oh come, Emmanuel.   Mediæval.   Translated by J. M. Neale.

Oh, could I speak the matchless worth.   Samuel Medley.

> The early life of Medley was very irreligious.   Being forgiven much, he loved much; and this is the sentiment of the hymn.

Oh, for a closer walk with God.   William Cowper, 1779.

Oh, for a heart to praise my God.   Charles Wesley, 1742.

Oh, for a thousand tongues, to sing.   Charles Wesley, 1739.   See page 225.

Oh, for the happy hour.

> Written by Rev. G. W. Bethune, while waiting for the arrival of his congregation, during a special effort to awaken a religious interest.

Oh, happy is the man who hears.   Michael Bruce.

Oh, how happy are they.   Charles Wesley.

Oh, mother dear, Jerusalem.   F. B. T.   See page 156.

> Translated by an unknown writer in the 16th century, and published from manuscript by Sir Roundell Palmer, in his " Book of Praise."

Oh, sing to me of. heaven.   Mrs. M. S. B. Dana.

Oh, that my load of sin were gone.   Charles Wesley.

Oh, the blood, the precious blood !
By Rev. G. H. Stockton, a Methodist minister.   Written. 1871.

Oh, where shall rest be found ?   James Montgomery.   See page 230.

Once in royal David's city.   Cecil Francis Alexander, 1848.
"Hymns for Little Children."

One sweetly solemn thought.   Phœbe Cary.   See page 206.

One there is above all others,   Newton.

On Jordan's bank the Baptist's cry.   Paris Breviary; translated by John
Chandler.

On Jordan's stormy banks I stand.
By Rev. Samuel Stennett, an English Baptist minister; born, 1727; died, 1795.

On the mountain-top appearing.   Kelly.   See page 137.

Onward, Christian soldiers.   Sabine Baring Gould.

O Paradise! O Paradise!   Frederick William Faber.   See page 189.

Oppressed with sin and woe.   Anne Bronte.
She was the youngest of three gifted sisters, whose home-life is known through the
memories of Charlotte Bronte.   She died young.   She said in her last sickness, "I
wish it would please God to spare me, because I long to do something good in the
world before I leave it."   Later in her sickness, she said, "It will be well through
the merits of the Redeemer."

O Thou, by long experience tried.   Madame Guyon.   See page 244.

O Thou from whom all goodness flows.   Thomas Haweis, 1792.
Mr. Haweis was one of Lady Huntingdon's chaplains, and one of the founders of the
London Missionary Society.   He wrote 256 hymns, which he published under the
title of " Carmina Christo."

O Thou, my soul, forget no more.   Krishnu-Pal.   See page 52.

O Thou to whom all creatures bow.   Tate and Brady.

O Thou to whose all-searching sight.   Tersteegen ; translated by John
Wesley.

O turn ye, O turn ye, for why will ye die.
Attributed to Samson Occom, the Indian preacher.

Our blest Redeemer, ere he breathed.   Harriet Auber, 1829.
Miss Auber led a secluded life, often expressing her religious thoughts in poems, only
a few of which were published.

Our God, our help in ages past.   Watts.   See page 222.

Parted many a toil-spent year.   See page 183.

Peace, troubled soul.   Shirley.   See page 126.

People of the living God.   James Montgomery.   See page 229.

Poor and afflicted, Lord, are thine.   Kelly.   See page 136.

Praise God, from whom all blessings flow.   Ken.   See page 17.

Prayer is appointed to convey.   Hart.

Prayer is the soul's sincere desire.   James Montgomery.

Quietly rest the woods and dales.   Gerhardt.   See page 85.

Rise, my soul, and stretch thy wings.   Robert Seagrave, 1742.
  Mr. Seagrave was a Calvinist Methodist in Lady Huntingdon's connection.

Rock of Ages, cleft for me.   Augustus Montague Toplady.   See page 24.

Salvation! O the joyful sound.   Isaac Watts.

Saviour, like a Shepherd lead us.   Anon.

Saviour, when in dust to thee.   Grant.

See how great a flame inspires.   Charles Wesley.   See page 226.

Shepherd of tender youth.   Anon.   See page 145.

Shout the glad tidings, exultingly sing.   W. A. Muhlenberg.   1826.

Show pity, Lord, O Lord, forgive.   Watts.   See page 224.

Shrinking from the cold hand of death.   Charles Wesley.

Shrinking from the cold hand of death,
  I soon shall gather up my feet;
Shall soon resign this fleeting breath,
  And die—my fathers' God to meet.
Numbered among thy people, I
  Expect with joy thy face to see :
Because thou didst for sinners die,
  Jesus, in death remember me !

Oh that, without a lingering groan,
  I may the welcome word receive;
My body with my charge lay down,
  And cease at once to work and live.
Walk with me through the dreadful shade,
  And, certified that thou art mine,
My spirit calm and undismayed
  I shall into thy hands resign.

No anxious doubt, no guilty gloom,
  Shall damp whom Jesus' presence cheers;
My Light, my Life, my God is come,
  And glory in his face appears.

The third stanza of this beautiful funeral hymn was an expression of Charles Wesley's feelings in regard to death.   John Wesley frequently quoted the stanza in old age. His almost constant prayer was, " Lord, let me not live to be useless."   " At every place," says Belcher, " after giving to his societies what he desired them to consider his last advice, he invariably concluded with the stanza beginning—
  " 'Oh that, without a lingering groan,
    I may the welcome word receive.' "

Sinners, turn, why will ye die?   Charles Wesley.

Softly now the light of day.   George Washington Doane, 1824.
" Songs by the Way."

Speed our republic, O Father on high ?

> M. Keller, the author of Keller's American hymn, is an adopted citizen of the United States.   During the war for the Union a prize was offered for a national hymn, and he felt a strong desire to produce such a composition for his adopted country.   It was first sung in New York, but awakened no interest.   Mr. Keller went to Boston, gave his hymn to the bands to play, and it soon became a favorite in that city, and was sung on all patriotic occasions where a large chorus was employed.   It was sung at the Peace Jubilee, at the reception of the battle flags at the Statehouse, by the request of Gov. Andrew, and by an adopted custom is the first piece played on the Common by bands on Independence days.

Stand up for Jesus.   Duffield.   See page 152.

Stand up, my soul, shake off thy fears.   Isaac Watts.

Stay, thou long-suffering Spirit, stay.   Charles Wesley.

Sun of my soul, thou Saviour dear.   John Keble.   See page 190

Sweet hour of prayer, sweet hour of prayer.

> This hymn was written by Rev. Mr. Walford, an English blind preacher, and was given to the public in 1849.   One of the stanzas of the original poem is usually omitted in American collections of hymns :
>
> > " Sweet hour of prayer, sweet hour of prayer.
> > The joy I feel, the bliss I share,
> > Of those whose anxious spirits burn
> > With strong desire for thy return ;
> > With such I hasten to the place
> > Where God, my Saviour, shows his face,
> > And gladly take my station there,
> > To wait for thee, sweet hour of prayer."

Sweet is the work, my God, my King.   Isaac Watts.

Sweet the moments, rich in blessing.   James Allen and Walter Shirley.
See page 127.

Take the name of Jesus with you.   Mrs. Lydia A. Baxter.

Te Deum Laudamus.

> The authorship of this very ancient hymn is commonly ascribed to St. Ambrose, who was born in Gaul about the year 340, and who was chosen Bishop of Milan in the year 374.   To him is attributed the introduction of singing antiphonal or responsive psalms into the Western church.   In reply to one who charged him with unduly influencing the minds of the people by the singing of hymns, he said: " A grand thing is that singing, and nothing can stand before it.   For what can be more telling than that confession of the Trinity which a whole population utters, day by day ?   For all are eager to proclaim their faith, and in measured strains have learned to confess Father, Son, and Holy Ghost."
>
> The Benedictine authors attribute to Ambrose twelve hymns.   St. Augustine thus

speaks of the effect produced upon him by the singing of the hymns of Ambrose in the church of Milan: "How did I weep, O Lord! through thy hymns and canticles, touched to the quick by the voices of thy sweet-attuned church! The voices sank into mine ears, and the truths distilled into my heart, whence the affections of my devotions overflowed; tears ran down, and I rejoiced in them."

The following is the English version of the hymn as it appears in the authorized book of Common Prayer:

We praise thee, O God, we acknowledge thee to be the Lord.

All the earth doth worship thee, the Father everlasting.

To thee all angels cry aloud, the heavens, and all the powers therein.

To thee cherubim and seraphim continually do cry,

Holy, Holy, Holy, Lord, God of Sabaoth;

Heaven and earth are full of the majesty of thy glory.

The glorious company of the apostles praise thee.

The goodly fellowship of the prophets praise thee.

The noble army of martyrs praise thee.

The holy church throughout all the world doth acknowledge thee,

The Father, of an infinite majesty;

Thine adorable, true, and only Son;

Also the Holy Ghost, the Comforter.

Thou art the King of Glory, O Christ;

Thou art the everlasting Son of the Father.

When thou tookest upon thee to deliver man, thou didst humble thyself to be born of a virgin;

When thou hadst overcome the sharpness of death, thou didst open the kingdom of heaven to all believers.

Thou sittest at the right hand of God, in the glory of the Father.

We believe that thou shalt come to be our Judge.

We therefore pray thee, help thy servants, whom thou hast redeemed with thy precious blood.

Make them to be numbered with thy saints in glory everlasting.

O Lord, save thy people, and bless thine heritage.

Govern them, and lift them up for ever.

Day by day we magnify thee;

And we worship thy name ever, world without end.

Vouchsafe, O Lord, to keep us this day without sin.

O Lord, have mercy upon us: have mercy upon us.

O Lord, let thy mercy be upon us, as our trust is in thee.

O Lord, in thee have I trusted; let me never be confounded.

Ten thousand times ten thousand.

This spirited hymn was written by Dean Henry Alford, widely known for his learned commentary, entitled "The Greek Testament with Notes." His first religious work was written at the age of ten, and was entitled "Looking unto Jesus." In his sixteenth year he formally dedicated himself wholly to the service of God, writing in his Bible this resolution: "I do this day, as in the presence of God and my own soul, renew my covenant with God, and solemnly determine henceforth to become his, and to do his work as far as in me lies."

In 1867 he issued a collection of hymns, of which fifty-five were of his own composition.

Ten thousand times ten thousand,
  In sparkling raiment bright,
The armies of the ransomed saints
  Throng up the steeps of light;
'T is finished, all is finished,
  Their fight with death and sin;
Fling open wide the golden gates,
  And let the victors in.

What rush of hallelujahs
  Fills all the earth and sky;
What ringing of a thousand harps
  Bespeaks the triumph nigh;

Oh day for which creation
  And all its tribes were made !
Oh joy for all its former woes
  A thousand-fold repaid !

Oh then what raptured greeting
  On Canaan's happy shore,
What knitting severed friendships up
  Where partings are no more !
Then eyes with joy shall sparkle
  That brimmed with tears of late,
Orphans no longer fatherless,
  Nor w dows desolate.

This hymn was sung at his own funeral service. On his tombstone was inscribed an impressive and beautiful line which he had written for the purpose :
    "The Inn of a Traveller on his Way to Jerusalem."

That Day of wrath, that dreadful day ! Walter Scott, 1805.

"Lay of the Last Minstrel." It was translated from the "Dies iræ, Dies illa." Scott repeated a part of the Latin original on his death-bed. See page 248.

The chariot ! the chariot ! its wheels roll in fire. Milman.

Dean Milman, a son of Sir Francis Milman, physician to George III., was born in 1791, and was educated at Oxford. In 1821 he was installed as University Professor of Poetry at Oxford, and it was while filling this position that he wrote this celebrated hymn, under the title of "The Last Day."

The day is past and gone. John Leland. See page 86.

"Elder" Leland was an eccentric Baptist minister, born in Grafton, Mass., 1754. Two verses from Watts, beginning, "And if we early rise," and "And when our days are past," are often added to this hymn in singing.

The God of Abram praise. Thomas Olivers. See page 234.

The heavens declare thy glory, Lord. Isaac Watts.

The King of glory we proclaim. James Montgomery. See page 231.

The Lord descended from above. Thomas Sternhold.

Scaliger declared that he wo ld rather be the author of the second stanza of this hymn than of all the works he had written.

The Lord my pasture shall prepare. Joseph Addison.

The sands of time are sinking. See page 93.

The spacious firmament on high. Joseph Addison.

The Spirit in our hearts. Henry Ustick Onderdonk.

The voice of free grace. Richard Bundsall. 1735–1824.

The world can neither give nor take. Lady Huntingdon. See page 102.

There is a happy land. Young. See page 146.

There is a fountain filled with blood.   William Cowper.

There is a land of pure delight.   Isaac Watts.   See page 221.

There is an hour of peaceful rest.   William B. Tappan.
> An assiduous Christian worker of Boston, long connected with the American Sunday-School Union.

There is an hour when I must part.
> This hymn was written in Switzerland by Rev. Andrew Reed, an English Congregationalist minister.   He said of it in his last days, "I wrote it at Geneva.   It has brought comfort to many, and now it brings comfort to me."

Thine earthly Sabbaths, Lord, we love.   Doddridge.   See page 34.

Thou art gone to the grave, but we will not deplore thee.   Bishop Heber.
> This hymn was written on the death of his brother.

Thou dear Redeemer, dying Lamb.   Cennick.   See page 56.

Thou hidden love of God, whose height.   Gerhard Tersteegen; translated by F. Wesley.   See page 162.

Thou shalt rise, my dust, thou shalt rise.   Klopstock.   See page 91.

Thou whose almighty word.   John Marriott, 1813.

Though nature's strength decay.   James Montgomery.   See page 236.

Thus far the Lord hath led me on.   Watts.

'T is finished; so the Saviour cried.   Samuel Stennett, 1787.

'T is my happiness below.   William Cowper.

'T is religion that can give.   Mary Masters.   See page 152.

To Jesus, the crown of my hope.   Cowper.   See page 48.

To leave my dear friends and with neighbors to part.   See page 49.

Unveil thy bosom, faithful tomb.   Watts.

Up to the hills I lift mine eyes.   Isaac Watts.

Veni, Sancte Spiritus.   Robert II.   See page 68.

Vital spark of heavenly flame.   Pope.   See page 62.

Watchman, tell us of the night.   John Bowring.   See page 128.

Welcome, sweet day of rest.   Isaac Watts.

We praise Thee, O God; we acknowledge Thee to be the Lord.   See page 262.

This is among the earliest a·d grandest tones in the Christian church, having probably been composed in the fourth century. It is the work of the Latin fathers, and is especially inscribed to Augustine and Ambrose. It appears in various forms in most ancient and modern collections, and is commonly known as the " Te Deum Laudamus."

We speak of the realms of the blest. Mrs. Mills. See page 148.

What are these in bright array? James Montgomery.

What shall a dying sinner do? Watts. See page 223.

When all thy mercies, O my God. Joseph Addison. See page 50.

When gathering clouds around I view. Robert Grant.

When I can read my title clear. Isaac Watts. See page 222.

When I survey the wondrous cross. Isaac Watts. See page 221.

When languor and disease invade. Toplady. See page 27.

When, marshalled on the nightly plain. Henry Kirke White. See page 132.

When shall we meet again? Alaric A. Watts.
   Written in youth, on parting from friends.

When shall we three meet again? See page 182.

When through the torn sail the wild tempest is streaming. Reginald Heber. See page 175.

When thou, my righteous Judge, shalt come. Lady Huntingdon. See page 104.

While shepherds watched their flocks by night. Nahum Tate.

While Thee I seek, Protecting Power. Helen Maria Williams. See page 129.

While with ceaseless course the sun. John Newton. See page 134.

Why do we mourn departing friends? Watts.

Why should the children of a King. Watts.

With one consent let all the earth. Tate and Brady.

Ye boundless realms of joy. Tate and Brady.

Ye choirs of New Jerusalem. St. Fulbert. See page 69.
   St. Fulbert was one of th: spiritual advisers of King Canute.

Ye virgin souls, arise. Charles Wesley. See page 108.

X. HYMN-WRITERS

AND THEIR HYMNS,

WITH THE PAGES OF THIS WORK, WHERE ANY OF THEM ARE REFERRED TO.

Abelard, Peter.　1079-1142.
> For the fount of life eternal.
> Ad perennis vitæ fontem.

Adam of S. Victor.　Died 1192.
> The church on earth with answering love.
> Supernæ matris gaudia.

Adams, John.　1751-1835.　Of Northampton, England.
> Jesus is our great salvation.

Adams, John Quincy.　1767-1848.
> How swift, alas! our moments fly.

Adams, Sarah Flower.　1805-1849.　See page 201.

Addiscott, Henry.　1806-1860.
> And is there, Lord, a cross for me?

Addison, Joseph.　1672-1719.　See pages 50, 98.

Alberti, Henry.　1604-1668.
> God who madest earth and heaven.
> Gott des Himmels und des Erden.

Alexander, Cecil Frances.　Born 1823.
> On Nebo's lofty mountain.
> The roseate hues of early dawn.

Alexander, Dr. William Lindsay.　1808.
> From distant corners of our land.

Alford, Dean Henry.　1810-1871.　See page 263.
> Ten thousand times ten thousand.

Allen, James.　1734-1804.　See Shirley, page 127.

Allen, G. N.

      Must Jesus bear the cross alone ?

Allen, Oswald. 1816.

      To-day thy mercy calls me.

Allendorf, John L. C. 1693–1773.

      Now rests her soul in Jesus' arms.
      Die Seele ruht in Jesu Armen.

Altenburg, See page 70.

      Fear not, O little flock, the foe.

Ambrose. 340–397.

      O Jesus, Lord of light and grace.
      Splendor paternæ gloriæ.

Anatolius, Saint. Died 458. See page 173.

Andrew, Saint (of Crete). 660–732.

      Oh, the mystery passing wonder.

Angelus, Silesius. 1624–1677.

      Oh Love, who formedst me to wear.
      Liebe, die du mich zum Bilde.

Anselm, Saint (of Lucca). Died 1086.

      Jesus, solace of my soul.
      Jesu mi dulcissime.

Anstice, Professor Joseph. 1808–1836.

      In all things like thy brethren Thou.

Apelles von Löwenstern. 1594–1648.

      O Christ ! the Leader of that war-worn host.
      Christe, du Beistand deiner Kreuzgemeine.

Aquinas, St. Thomas. 1227–1274.

      Now, my tongue, the mystery telling.

Auber, Harriet. 1773–1862.

      Our blest Redeemer, ere he breathed.

Austin, John. Died 1669.

      Blest be thy love, dear Lord.

Aveling, Thomas W. 1815.

      On ! towards Zion, on !

Bache, Mrs. 1744–1808.

      See how He loved.

Bacon, Leonard. 1802.

      Wake the song of jubilee!

Bahnmaier, J. F. 1774–1841.

Baker, H. W. 1821.
> Oh, what, if we are Christ's.

Bakewell, John. 1721–1819.
> Hail! thou once-despised Jesus.

Baldwin, Thomas. 1753–1825.
> Come, happy souls, adore the Lamb.

Balfour, Alex. 1767–1829.
> Go, messengers of peace and love.

Bancroft, C. L. Ireland.
> Oh, for the robes of whiteness.

Barbauld, Anna Letitia. 1744–1825.
> Praise to God, immortal praise.

Baring-Gould, Sabine. See page 154.
> Onward, Christian soldiers.

Barton, Bernard. 1784–1849.
> Lamp of our feet, whereby we trace.

Bateman, Henry. 1800.
> Let us with a cheerful voice.

Bathurst, W. H. 1796.
> Oh, for a faith that will not shrink.

Baxter, Lydia. 1809–1874.
> There is a gate that stands ajar.

Baxter, Richard. 1615–1691.
> Lord, it belongs not to my care.

Bede. 672–735.

Beddome, B. 1717–1795. See page 138.
> Did Christ o'er sinners weep?

Beecher, Charles. 1819.
> We are on our journey home.

Benedictis, J. De. Died 1306.
> At the cross her station keeping.
> Stabat mater dolorosa.

Bennet, S. F.
> There's a land that is fairer than day

Bernard, St. 1091–1153 (of Clairvaux).

Bernard, St. Born 1150 (of Cluny).
> Brief life is here our portion.
> Hic brevé vivitur.
> Jerusalem the golden.
> Urbs Syon aurea.

23*

Berridge, John. 1716–1793.
> O happy saints, who dwell in light.

Bethune, George W. 1805–1862.

Bienemann, C. 1540–1591.
> Come, O my soul, in sacred lays.

Bilby, Thomas. Born 1794–1872.
> Here we suffer grief and pain.

Binney, Thomas. Born about 1798.
> Eternal Light! eternal Light!

Birks, T. Rawson. 1810.
> Oh, covenant Angel, full of grace.

Blackie, Professor J. S. 1809.
> Angels holy, high and lowly.

Blacklock, Dr. Thomas. 1721–1791.
> Come, O my soul, in sacred lays.

Blair, Robert. 1699–1746.
> What though no flowers the fig-tree clothe.

Blew, William John.
> The day is past and gone; Great, etc.

Bliss, P. P. 1838.
> Almost persuaded now to believe.

Blunt, R. W.
> Jesus, thy blessed brow is torn.

Bode, John Ernest. 1816.
> Thou, who hast called us by thy word.

Boden, James. 1757–1841.
> Ye dying sons of men.

Bonar, Dr. Horatius. 1808. See page 194.

Bonaventura, Saint. 1221-1274.
> In the Lord's atoning grief.
> In passione Domini.

Borthwick, Jane. 1854.
> My Jesus, as thou wilt.
> Mein Jesu, wie du willst.

Bottome, Rev. F. 1870.
> O bliss of the purified, bliss of the free.

Bourignon, Antoinette. 1616–1680.
> Come, Saviour Jesus, from above.
> Venez Jésus. mon salutaire.

Bowdler, John. 1783–1815.
> Lord, before thy throne we bend.

Bowring, Sir John. 1792–1872. See page 128.

Brackenbury, R. Carr. 1752–1818.
> Come, Holy Spirit, raise our songs.

Bradberry, David. 1735–1803.
> Now let our hearts conspire to raise.

Brady, Dr. Nicholas. 1659–1726.

Brewer, Jehoida. 1752–1817.
> Hail, sovereign love, that first began.

Bridges, Matthew. Born about 1802.
> Crown Him with many crowns.

Brontë, Anne. 1820–1849.

Brown, Phœbe II. 1783–1861. See page 48.

Brown, William.
> Welcome, sacred day of rest.

Browne, Simon. 1680–1732.
> Come, gracious Spirit, heavenly Dove.

Browne, Sir Thomas. 1605–1682.
> The night is come; like to the day.

Bruce, Michael. 1746–1767.
> Where high the heavenly temple stands.

Bryant, William Cullen. Born 1794.
> Deem not that they are blest alone.

Bubier, Professor G. B. 1823.
> I would commune with thee, my God.

Buckoll, Henry J.
> Word of Him whose sovereign will.
> Walte, walte, nah und fern,
> Allgewaltig Wort des Herrn.

Bulfinch, Stephen Greenleaf. 1809–1870.
> Hail to the Sabbath-day !

Bullock, Dr. William.
> We love the place, O God.

Bulmer, Agnes. 1775–1837.
> Thou who hast in Zion laid.

Bulmer, John. 1784–1857.
> Lord of the vast creation.

Bunting, William Maclardie. 1805–1866.
> O God ! how often hath thine ear.

Bürde, Samuel Gottlieb. 1753–1831.
> Come, happy souls, adore the Lamb.

Burder, George. 1752–1832.
> Great the joy when Christians meet.

Burgess, Bishop George. 1809–1866.
> When forth from Egypt's trembling strand.

Burleigh, William Henry. 1812-1871.
> Through the changes of the day.

Burnham, Richard. 1749–1810.
> Jesus ! thou art the sinner's Friend.

Burns, James Drummond. 1823–1864.
> Still with thee, O my God.

Burton, John, Sen. 1773–1822.
> Time is winging us away.
> Holy Bible, book divine.

Burton, John. Jr. 1803.
> Pilgrims we are, and strangers.

Butcher, Edmund. 1757–1822.
> Great God, as seasons disappear.

Butterworth, Joseph Henry.
> Spirit of Wisdom ! guide thine own.

Byrom, John. 1691–1763.
> Christians, awake, salute the happy morn.

Caddell, Cecelia Mary.
> It is finished ! He hath wept.

Calvin, John. 1500–1564.
> I greet thee, who my sure Redeemer.

Cambridge, Ada. 1844.
> Humbly now, with deep contrition.

Cameron, William. 1751–1811.
> How bright these glorious spirits shine.

Campbell, Robert. Died, 1868.
> At the Lamb's high feast we sing.
> Ad regias Agni dapes.

Campbell, Thomas. 1777–1844.
> When Jordan hushed his waters still.

Canitz, F. R. L., Baron von. 1654–1699.
> Come, my soul, thou must be waking.
> Seele, du musst munter werden.

Carlyle, J. Dacre. 1759–1804.
> Lord, when we bend before thy throne.

Carpenter, Dr. Joseph E. 1813.
> Lord and Father of creation.

Caswall, Edward. 1814.
> Jesus, the very thought of thee.

Cawood, John. 1775–1852.
> Almighty God ! thy word is cast.

Cennick, John. 1717–1755. See page 54.

Chambers, J. David.
> Exult, all hearts, with gladness.
> Exultet cor præcordiis.

Chandler, John. 1806.
> Christ is our corner-stone.

Charles, Mrs. Elizabeth.
> Never farther than Thy cross.

Churton, Archdeacon Edward. 1800.
> God of grace, O let thy light.

Clarke, J. Freeman. 1810.
> Hast thou wasted all the powers.

Clausnitzer, Tobiah. 1619–1684.
> Gracious Jesus ! in thy name.
> Liebster Jesu, wir sind hier.

Clayton, George. 1783–1862.
> From yon delusive scene.

Clemens, Alexandrinus, Saint. Died about 217.
> Shepherd of tender youth.

Cobbin, Ingram. 1777–1851.
> If 't is sweet to mingle where.

Codner, Elizabeth. 1860.
> Lord, I hear of showers of blessing.

Coffin, Charles. 1676–1749.
> Creator of the world, to thee.
> Te læta, mundi Creator.

Collins, Henry.
>> Jesus, meek and lowly.

Collyer, Dr. W. Bengo.   1782–1854.
>> Return, O wanderer, return.

Conder, Josiah.   1789–1855.
>> O thou God, who hearest prayer.
>> When I can trust my all with God.

Conder, Joan Elizabeth.
>> The hours of evening close.

Cook, Russell Salmon.   1814–1864.
>> Just as thou art, without one trace.

Cook, Mrs. M. A. W.   See page 252.
>> In some way or other the Lord will provide.

Cooper, J.
>> Father of heaven, whose love profound.

Copeland, William J.
>> Jesus, the world's redeeming Lord.
>> Jesu, Salvator sæculi.

Cosin, Bishop.   1594–1672.
>> Come, Holy Ghost, our souls inspire.
>> Veni, Creator Spiritus.

Cosmas, Saint.   Died, 760.
>> Christ is born! exalt his name.

Cotterill, Thomas.   1779–1823.
>> O'er the realms of pagan darkness.

Cottle, Joseph.   1770–1853.
>> From every earthly pleasure.

Cotton, Dr. Nathaniel.   1707–1788.
>> Affliction is a stormy deep.

Cowper, William.   1731–1800.   See pages 44 and 47.

Coxe, Bishop Arthur Cleveland.   1818.
>> How beauteous were the marks divine.

Crabbe, George.   1754–1832.
>> Pilgrim, burdened with thy sin.

Crewdson, Jane.   1809–1863.
>> There is no sorrow, Lord, too light.

Croly, Dr. George.   1780–1860.
>> Behold me, Lord, and if thou find.

Croswell, William. 1804-1854.
>> Lead, lead the way, the Saviour.

Crosby, Fanny J. Born 1823.
>> Safe in the arms of Jesus.

Crossman, Samuel. 1624-1683.
>> Sweet place, sweet place alone.

Cummins, James J. Died, 1867.
>> Shall hymns of grateful love.

Dale, Thomas. 1797.
>> Dear as thou wert, and justly dear.

Damiani, Peter. 988-1072.
>> For the fount of life eternal.
>> Ad perennis vitæ fontem.

Dana, Mrs. M. S. B. 1850.
>> O sing to me of heaven.

Darby, John Nelson.
>> Rise, my soul, thy God directs thee.

Davies, Samuel. 1724-1761.
>> Great God of wonders, all thy ways.

Davis, Thomas.
>> Sing, ye seraphs in the sky.

Dayman, Edward Arthur.
>> O splendor of the Father's might.
>> Splendor paternæ gloriæ.

Deacon, Samuel. 1746-1816.
>> To Jordan's streams the Saviour.

Decius, Nicholas. Died, 1529.
>> To God on high be thanks and praise.
>> Allein Gott, in der Höh', sei Ehr.

Deck, James George. Born 1802.
>> It is thy hand, my God.

De Courcy, Richard. 1743-1803.
>> Jesus, at thy command.

De Fleury, Maria. 1791. Her Hymns and Poems uppeared 1791.
>> Come, saints, and adore Him, come bow at His feet.

Denny, Sir Edward. 1796.
>> Light of the lonely pilgrim's heart.

Dent, Caroline.
> Jesus, Saviour! thou dost know.

Dessler, W. C. 1660–1722.
> Jesus, whose glory's streaming rays.
> Mein Jesu, dem die Seraphinen.

Dickson, David. 1583–1662. See page 156.
> O mother dear, Jerusalem.

Dickinson, William. 1816–1868.
> When the gospel race is run.

Dix, William Chatterton. 1837.
> As with gladness, men of old.

Doane, Bishop G. W. 1799–1859.
> Thou art the Way! to thee alone.

Dobell, John. 1757–1840.

Dober, Anna. 1713–1739.
> Holy Lamb, who thee receive.

Doddridge, Dr. Philip. 1702–1751. See page 34.

Downton, Henry. Born 1818.
> For thy mercy and thy grace.

Dracup, John. Died, 1795.
> Thanks to thy name, O Lord, that we.

Drennan, William. 1754–1820.
> The heaven of heavens cannot contain.

Dryden, John. 1632–1700.
> Creator, Spirit! by whose aid.

Duffield, George. 1818. See page 153.

Duncan, Mary Lundie. 1814–1840.

Dwight, Timothy. 1752–1817. See page 252.

Eber, Paul. 1511–1569.
> When in the hour of utmost need.
> Wenn wir in höchster Noth und Pein.

Edmeston, James. 1791–1867. See page 165.

Elizabeth, Charlotte, (Tonna.) 1790–1846.
> Rose of Sharon, far excelling

Elliott, Charlotte. See page 155.

Elliott, Julia A. Died, 1841.
> We love thee, Lord, yet not alone.

Elven, Cornelius.   1797.
>> With broken heart and contrite sigh.

Enfield, Dr. William.   1741–1797.
>> Behold, where in a mortal form.

England, Samuel S.   1810.
>> In anger, Lord, rebuke me not.

Ephrem, Syrus.   Died, 381.
>> To thee, O Lord, loud praise ascendeth.

Evans, James Harrington.   1785–1840.
>> Change is our portion here.

Evans, Jonathan.   1749–1809.
>> Come, thou soul-transforming Spirit.

Faber, Dr. Frederick W.   1815–1863.   See page 187.

Fanch, James.   1704–1767.
>> Beyond the glittering starry sky.

Fawcett, Dr. John.   1739–1817.   See page 37.

Fellows, John.   Wrote about 1773.   Died 1785.
>> Great God! now condescend.

Fletcher, Samuel.   1785–1863.
>> Father of life and light.

Flowerdew, Alice.   1759–1830.
>> Fountain of mercy, God of love.

Fortunatus, V. H. C.   530–609.
>> The royal banners forward go.
>> Vexilla regis prodeunt.

Fountain, John.   Born 1767.   Died, 1800.
>> Sinners, you are now addressed.

Francis, Benjamin.   1734–1799.
>> My gracious Redeemer I love.

Frank, John.   1618–1677.
>> Jesus, my chief pleasure.
>> Jesu, meine Freude.

Frank, Solomon.   1659–1725.
>> So rest, my Rest.
>> So ruhest du, O meine Ruh'

Frelinghuysen, J. A.   1670–1739.
>> The day is gone.
>> Der Tag ist hin.

Fulbert, Saint, (of Chartres.)   Died about 1029.   See page 69.

Gabb, James.
>Jesus, thou wast once a child.

Gandy, Samuel Whitlock.   Died about 1858.
>His be the " victor's name."

Gascoigne, George.   Died, 1577.
>We that have passed in slumber sweet.

Gellert, C. Fürchtegott.   1715–1769.
>Jesus lives, no longer now.
>Jesus lebt, mit Ihm auch .ch.

Gerhardt, Paul.   1606–1676.   See page 80.

Gesenius, Dr. Justus.   1601–1671.
>O Lord, when condemnation.
>Wenn mich die Sünden kränken.

Geste, Guillaumede.
>The Shepherd now was smitten.
>Pastore percusso, minas.

Gibbons, Dr. Thomas.   1720–1785.
>Now let our souls on wings sublime.

Gilbert, Ann.   1782–1866.
>Oh, happy they, who safely housed.

Giles, John Eustace.   1805–1875.
>Hast thou said, exalted Jesus ?   1837.

Godescalcus.   Died about 950.
>The strain upraise of joy and praise.   Alleluia !
>Cantemus cuncti melodum.   Alleluia !

Goode, William.   1762–1816.
>Thou, gracious God, and kind.

Gough, Benjamin.   1805.
>Awake ! awake ! O Zion.

Grant, James.   Died, 1785.
>O Zion, afflicted with wave upon wave.

Grant, Sir Robert.   1785–1838.
>Oh, worship the King.

Greene, Thomas.   1785.
>It is the Lord—enthroned in light.

Gregor, Christian.   1723–1801.
>Man of sorrows, and acquainted.

Gregory the Great. 550–604.
> Father of mercies, hear !
> Audi, benigne Conditor.

Greville, Dr. R. K. 1794–1866.
> O God, from thee alone.

Grigg, Joseph. Died, 1768. See page 60.

Guest, Benjamin. Died, 1869.
> Heavenly Father, may thy love.

Guiet, Charles. Died about 1684.
> O Word of God above.
> Patris Æterni soboles coeva.

Gunn, H. Mayo. Born 1818.
> To realms beyond the sounding sea.

Gurney, Archer T. 1820.
> Memory of the blest departed.

Gurney, John Hampden. 1802–1862.
> Lord, as to thy dear cross we flee.

Guyon, Jeanne B. de la Motte. 1648–1717. See page 237.
Harmer, J. Y.
> In the Christian's home in glory.

Hall, Mrs. E. M.
> I hear the Saviour say.

Hall, C. Newman. 1816.
> Hallelujah ! joyful raise.

Hamilton, Dr. R. Winter. 1794–1848.
> Though poor in lot, and scorned in name.

Hammond, William. Died, 1783.
> Awake, and sing the song.

Hankey, Kate.
> I love to tell the story.

Harland, Edward. Born 1809.
> Lord, when earthly comforts flee.

Harris, Dr. John. 1802–1856.
> Light up this house with glory, Lord.

Hart, Joseph. 1712–1768. See page 35.

Hastings, Dr. Thomas. 1784. This hymn was written by the Rev. S. F. Smith, D. D., and altered by Dr. Hastings.
> To-day the Saviour calls .

Hatfield, Edwin F.   1807.
> My Shepherd's name is love.

Havergal, William Henry.   1793.
> Hosanna! raise the pealing hymn.

Havergal, F. R.   See page 169.
> I gave my life for thee.

Haweis, Dr. Thomas.   1732–1820.
> O Thou, from whom all goodness flows.
> From the cross uplifted high.

Hawks, Mrs. A. S.   Born 1835.
> I need thee every hour.

Hawkesworth, Dr. John.   1715–1773.
> In sleep's serene oblivion laid.

Hawkins, Ernest.   1802–1868.
> Lord, the Saviour's love displaying.

Hayn, H. Louisa von.   1724–1782.
> Seeing I am Jesus' lamb.
> Weil ich Jesu Schüflein bin.

Heber, Bishop Reginald.   1783–1826.   See page 40.

Heginbothom, Ottiwell.   1744–1768.
> God of our life! thy various praise.

Hemans, Felicia D.   1794–1835.
> Lowly and solemn be.

Herbert, George.   1593–1632.
> Teach me, my God and King.

Herbert, Daniel.   1751–1833.
> Come, dear Lord, thyself reveal.

Hermann, Nicholas.   Died 1561.
> Mine hour appointed is at hand.
> Wann mein Stündlein vorhanden ist.

Herrick, Robert.   1591.
> In the hour of my distress.

Hervey, James.   1714–1758.
> Since all the downward tracks of time.

Hewett, John William.
> O Thou who dost to man accord.

Hildebert, Archbishop.   Died 1133.

Hildegarde, Saint.   1098–1179.
> O Fire of God, the Comforter.
> O ignis Spiritus Paracleti.

Hill, Rowland.   1744–1833.
> Ye that in his courts are found.

Hinds, Bishop Samuel.   1793.
> Lord, shall thy children come to thee ?

Hinton, J. Howard.   1791–1872.
> Once I was estranged from God.

Hogg, James.   1772–1835.
> O Thou that dwellest in the heavens high.

Hojer, Conrad.   Sixteenth century.
> Jesus, my only God and Lord.

Homburg, Ernest C.   1605–1681.
> Of my life the life, O Jesus,
> Jesu, meines Lebens Leben.

Horne, Bishop George.   1730–1792.
> See the leaves around us falling.

Hoskins, Joseph.   Died 1788.
> The time is short ere all who live.

How, William Walsham.   1823.
> Jesus ! name of wondrous love.

Huie, Dr. Richard.   1795.
> O ye, who with the silent tear.

Hull, Amelia Matilda.   1860.
> There is life for a look at the Crucified One.

Humphreys, Joseph.   1720.
> Blessed are the sons of Go '.

Huntingdon, Selina, Countess of.   1707–1791.   See page 101.

Hupton, Job.   1762–1849.
> Come, ye faithf l, raise the anthem.

Hurn, William.   1754-1829.
> Rise, gracious God, and shine.

Huss, John.   1373–1415.
> Jesus Christ, our true salvation.
> Jesus Christus, nostra salus.

24*

Hutton, James.   1715–1795.
> O teach us more of thy blest ways.

Hyde, Ann Beadley.   Died 1872.
> And canst thou, sinner, slight ?

Ingemann, Bernhardt Severin.   1789–1862.

Irons, Joseph.   1785–1852.
> Plead my cause, O Lord of hosts.

Irons, Dr. William J.   1812.
> Day of wrath, O day of mourning.

Jervis, Thomas.   1748–1833.
> Lord of the world's majestic frame.

John, St. Damascene.   Died about 780.
> 'T is the day of resurrection.

Jones, Edmund.   Born 1722.   Died 1765.
> Come, humble sinner, in whose breast.

Joseph, Saint, (of the Studium.)   Ninth century.
> Let our choirs new anthems raise.

Jowett, William.
> While conscious sinners tremble.

Joyce, James.   1781–1850.
> Oh why should Israel's sons, once blest.

Judson, Dr. Adoniram.   1788–1850.
> Our Father, God, who art in heaven.

Keble, John.   1792–1866.   See page 190.

Kelly, Thomas.   1769–1855.   See page 135.

Ken, Bishop Thomas.   1637–1711.   See page 17.

Kennedy, Dr. B. Hall.   1804.
> Come, Lord Jesus, take thy rest.

Kent, John.   1766–1843.
> Where two or three together meet.

Killinghall, John.   Died 1740.
> In all my troubles sharp and strong.

Kingsbury, William.   1744–1818.
> Great Lord of all thy churches, hear.

Kippis, Dr. Andrew.   1725–1795.
> With grateful hearts, with joyful tongues.

Klopstock, F. G.   1724–1803.   See page 86.

Knapp, Albert.   1798–1864.
> O Father, thou who hast created all.
> O Vaterherz, das Erd' und Himmel schuf.

Knorr, von Rosenroth Christian.   1636–1689.
> Come, thou bright and morning Star.

Koitsch, C. J.   Died 1735.
> O Fountain eternal of life and of light.
> O Ursprung des Lebens, O ew'ges Licht.

Kynaston, Dr. Herbert.   1809.
> Jesus, solace of my soul.
> Jesu mi dulcissime, Domine cœlorum.

Lagniel, John.   Died 1728.
> Doth He who came the lost to seek.

Langbecker, E. C. G.   1792–1843.
> What shall I be, my Lord, when I behold thee.
> Wie wird mir sein, wenn ich dich, Jesu, sehe.

Lange, Ernest.   1650–1727.
> O God ! thou bottomless abyss.
> O Gott, du Tiefe sonder Grund.

Lange, Joachim.   1670–1744.
> O God ! what offering shall I give ?
> Was soll ich denn nun, mein Gott, zum Opfer schenken ?

Langford.
> Now begin the heavenly theme.

Laurenti, Laurentius.   1660–1722.
> Rejoice, rejoice, believers.
> Ermuntert euch, ihr Frommen.

Lavater, John Caspar.   1741–1801.
> O name, than every name more dear.
> O süssester der Namen all.

Lee, Miss M. A.
> I am far frae my hame, an' I'm weary oftenwhiles.

Lee, Dr. Frederick George.   Died 1868.
> Laud the grace of God victorious.

Leeson, Jane E.   Died 1853.
> Their hearts shall not be moved.

Liguori, Saint Alphonso.   1696–1787.
> My Jesus, say what wretch has dared.

Lingley, James.
> Once more we leave the busy road.

Littledale, Richard Frederick.

Lloyd, William Freeman. 1791–1853.
> Our times are in thy hand.

Logan, John. 1748–1788.

Longfellow, Henry Wadsworth. 1807.
> Tell me not in mournful numbers.
> There is no flock, however watched and tended.
> Into the Silent Land. (Translation.)

Louisa Henrietta (of Brandenburg). 1627–1667.
> Jesus, my Redeemer, lives.
> Jesus, meine Zuversicht.

Lowry, Rev. R. Born 1826.
> Shall we gather at the river ?

Luke, Jemima. 1813. See page 146.

Luther, Martin. 1483–1546. See page 15.

Lynch, Thomas Tolse. 1818–1871.
> Mountains by the darkness hidden.

Lyte, Henry Francis. 1793–1847. See page 211.

McCheyne, Robert Murray. 1813–1843.

Macduff, Dr. John Robert.
> Oh do not, blessed Lord, depart.

Mackay, Margaret. 1832.
> Asleep in Jesus, blessed sleep.

Madan, Martin. 1726–1790.

Manly, Basil, Jr. 1825.
> Holy, holy, holy, Lord.

Mant, Bishop Richard. 1776–1848.
> Praise the Lord, ye heavens, adore him.

March, Henry. Born about 1790.
> Oh send thy light, thy truth, my God.

Mardley, John. Died 1562.

Maria, Queen of Hungary. 1505–1558.
> Can I my fate no more withstand ?

Montgomery, James. 1771–1854. See page 227.

Moore, Thomas. 1779–1852.
>Come, ye disconsolate, where'er ye languish.

More, Henry. 1614–1687.
>Father, if justly still we claim.

Morell, Thomas. 1781–1840.
>Father of mercies, condescend.

Morris, Eliza Fanny. 1821.
>God of pity, God of grace.

Morrison, Dr. John. 1749–1798.
>The race that long in darkness pined.

Mott, Edward. Born 1797.
>My hope is built on nothing less.

Moultrie, Gerard.
>Brother, now thy toils are o'er.

Moultrie, Mary Dunlop.
>Agnes, fair martyr.

Muhlenburg, W. A. 1796. See page 254.
>I would not live always.

Naur, Elias Eskillsen.
>When my tongue can no more.
>Naar min Tunge ikke mere.

Neale, J. Mason. 1818–1866.
>Jerusalem the Golden. (Translation.)
>Brief life is here our portion. (Translation.)

Neander, Joachim. 1640–1680.
>Behold me here in grief draw near.
>Sieh, hier bin ich Ehren-König.

Needham, John. 1710–1768.
>To praise the ever-bounteous Lord.

Neumark, George. 1621–1681.
>Leave God to order all thy ways.
>Wer nur den lieben Gott lässt walten.

Nevin, Edwin H. 1814.
>Always with me! always with me!

Newman, Dr. John Henry. 1801. See pages 215, 257.
>Lead, kindly light.

Nicholas, Tressilian G. Born about 1823.
> Lord, when before thy throne we meet.

Nicolai, Dr. Philip. 1556–1608.
> Wake, ye holy maidens, fearing.
> Wachet auf, ruft uns die Stimme.

Newton, James. 1733–1790.
> Let plenteous grace descend on those.

Newton, John. 1725–1807. See page 177.

Noel, Hon. B. Wriotheseley. 1799–1873.

Noel, Hon. Gerard Thomas. 1782–1851.
> If human kindness meets return.

Nunn, Marianne. 1799–1848.
> One there is above all others.

Nyberg, L. T. 1720–1792.
> Father, throned on high.

Oberlin, John Frederick. 1740–1826.
> O Lord, thy heavenly grace impart.

Odo, Saint, (of Cluny.) 879–942.
> O Church, our mother, speak His praise.
> Lauda, mater ecclesia.

Olivers, Thomas. 1725–1799. See page 234.

Onslow, Phipps.
> Hark! a glad exulting throng.
> Christi caterva clamitat.

Opie, Amelia. 1769–1853.
> There seems a voice in every gale.

Osler, Edward. 1798–1863.
> Great God, o'er heaven and earth supreme.

Oswald, Henry Sigismund. 1751–1837.
> O let him whose sorrow.
> Wem in Leidenstagen.

Palgrave, Francis Turner. 1824.
> Star of morn and even.

Palmer, Dr. Ray. 1808. See page 209.

Park, Thomas. 1760–1835.
> My soul, praise the Lord, speak good of his namo.

Parr, Harriet.
> Hear my prayer, O heavenly Father.

Parson, Elizabeth.　1812.
>　　　　Jesus, we love to meet.

Paulus, Diaconus.　Died about 799.
>　　Greatest of prophets, messenger appointed.
>　　Ut queant laxis resonare fibris.

Peabody, Dr. W. B. O.　1799–1848.
>　　Behold the western evening sky.

Pearce, Samuel.　1766–1799.
>　　In the floods of tribulation.

Perronet, Edward.　Died 1792.　See page 13.

Phillimore, Greville.
>　　O Lord of health and life, what tongue can tell.

Pierpont, John.　1785–1866.
>　　O Thou, to whom in ancient time.

Pope, Alexander.　1688–1744.　See page 62.

Pott, Francis.
>　　Alleluia! Alleluia! Alleluia!

Prudentius, A. Clemens.　348.　Died about 413.
>　　Earth has many a noble city.
>　　O sola magnarum urbium.

Prynne, G. Rundle.　1860.
>　　Jesus, meek and gentle.

Pyer, John.　1799–1859.
>　　Met again in Jesus' name.

Rabanus, Maurus, Saint.　776–856.
>　　Christ, of the holy angels light and gladness.
>　　Christe, sanctorum decus angelorum.

Raffles, Dr. Thomas.　1788–1863.
>　　Lord, like the publican I stand.

Rawson, George.　1807.
>　　Father of love and power.

Reed, Dr. Andrew.　1787–1862.　See page 265.
>　　There is an hour when I must part.

Reed, Elizabeth.　1794–1867.
>　　My longing spirit faints to see.

Rhodes, Benjamin.　1743–1815.
>　　My heart and voice I raise.

Richter, C. F.   1676–1711.
Thou Lamb of God, thou Prince of Peace.

Ringwaldt, Bartholomew.   1530–1598.
Great God! what do I see and hear?

Rinkart, Martin.   1586–1649.
Now thank we all our God.
Nun danket alle Gott.

Rippon, Dr. John.   1751–1836.
Great God, where'er we pitch our tent.

Robert II., (of France.)   972–1031.   See page 67.

Robertson, William.   Died 1743.
The Saviour comes, no outward pomp.

Robinson, Robert.   1735–1790.   See page 42.

Rorison, Dr. Gilbert.   1821–1869.
Three in One, and One in Three.

Roscommon, Earl of.   Died 1684.
The last loud trumpet's wondrous sound.

Rossetti, Christina G.   1850.
What are these that glow from afar?

Rothe, John A.   1688–1758.
Now have I found the ground wherein.
Ich habe nun den Grund gefunden.

Russell, Arthur Tozer.   1806.
O God of life, whose power benign.

Russell, William.
More marred than any man's.

Ryland, Dr. John.   1753–1825.
Sovereign Ruler of the skies.

Saffery, Maria Grace.   1773–1858.
'Tis the great Father we adore.

Sandys, George.   1577–1643.
Sing the great Jehovah's praise.

Santolius, Maglorianus.   1628–1684.
Now, my soul, thy voice upraising.
Prome vocem, meus, canoram.

Santolius, Victorinus.   1630–1697.
Disposer Supreme.
Supreme quales Arbiter.   ·

Scales, Thomas. 1786–1860.

> Amazing was the grace.

Schenk, H. Theodore. Died 1727.

> Who are these like stars appearing !
> Wer sind die vor Gottes Throne.

Schmolke, Benjamin. 1672-1737.

Scholefield, Professor James. 1789–1853.

> My Jesus, as thou wilt!
> Mein Jesu, wie Du willst.

Schröder, J. H. 1666–1699.

> Wisdom's unexhausted treasure.
> Aller Weisheit höchste Fülle.

Schütz, John Jacob. 1640–1690.

> All praise and thanks to God Most High.
> Sei Lob und Ehr dem höchsten.

Scott, Robert Allan.

> All glory be to Thee.

Scott, Thomas. Died about 1776.

> Angels, roll the rock away
> Hasten, sinners, to be wise.

Seagrave, Robert. 1693.

> Rise, my soul, and stretch thy wings.

Sears, Edmund H. 1810.

> It came upon the midnight clear.

Sedulius, Coelius. Fifth century.

> Why doth that impious Herod fear.
> Hostis Herodes impie.

Serle, Ambrose. 1742–1812.

> Thy ways, O Lord, with wise design.

Seymour, A. C. Hobart. 1789.

> Awake, all-conquering Arm, awake!

Shepherd, Anne. Born 1809. Died 1857.

> Around the throne of God in heaven.

Shepherd, Thomas. 1665–1739.

> When wilt thou come unto me, Lord ?

Shipton, Anna.

> Jesus, Master, hear my cry!

Shirley, Hon. Walter. 1725–1786. See page 123.

Shrubsole, William, Jr.   1759–1829.
>> Arm of the Lord, awake, awake!

Sigourney, Lydia Huntley.   1792–1865.
>> Saviour, thy law we love.

Simpson, Jane Cross.
>> Go when the morning shineth.

Smith, Dr. George.   1803–1870.
>> Thou art, O Christ, the way.

Smith, Sir James Edward.   1759–1828.
>> Adore, my soul, that awful Name.

Smith, Joseph Denham.   Born about 1816.
>> Just as Thou art—how wondrous fair!

Smith, Dr. Samuel F.   1809.   See page 257.

Smyttan, George Hunt.
>> Forty days and forty nights.

Southey, Caroline Anne.   1786–1854.
>> I weep, but not rebellious tears.

Spangenburg, Augustus G.   1704–1792.
>> What shall we offer our good Lord ?
>> Der König ruht, und schauet doch.

Spitta, Dr. Charles J. P.   1801–1859.
>> See, oh see, what love the Father.

Spurgeon, Charles Hadden.   1834.
>> The Holy Ghost is here.

Stammers, Joseph.   1801.
>> Breast the wave, Christian, when it is strongest.

Stanley, Dean Arthur Penrhyn.   1815.
>> He is gone, and we remain.

Steele, Anne.   1716–1778.   See page 58.

Stennett, Dr. Joseph.   1663–1713.

Stennett, Dr. Samuel.   1727–1795.
>> On Jordan's stormy banks I stand.

Stephen, Saint, (the Sabaite.)   725–794.   See page 246.
>> Art thou weary, art thou languid.

Sternhold, Thomas.   Died 1549.
>> O God, my strength and fortitude.

Stocker, John.   About 1776.
>> Gracious Spirit, Dove divine.

Stockton, Rev. G. H.
> Oh the blood. the precious blood.

Stowe, Harriet E. Beecher.   1814.   See page 256.

Stowell, Canon Hugh.   1799–1865.   See page 249.

Straphan, Joseph.   1757.
> Blest work, the youthful mind to win.

Swain, Joseph.   1761–1796.
> How sweet, how heavenly is the sight!

Swaine, Edward.   1795–1862.
> Lord Jesus, let thy watchful care.

Tappan, William Bingham.   1794–1849.
> There is an hour of peaceful rest.

Tate, Nahum.   1652–1715.
> While shepherds watched their flocks by night.

Tauler, John.   1294–1361.
> There comes a galley sailing.
> Es kommt ein Schiff geladen.

Taylor, Clare.   Died 1778.
> What wondrous cause could move thy heart ?

Taylor, Jane.   1783–1824.
> Great God, and wilt thou condescend ?

Taylor, Jeremy.   1613–1667.
> Draw near to thy Jerusalem, O Lord.

Taylor, T. Rawson.   1807–1835,   See page 159.

Tersteegen, Gerhard.   1697–1769.   See page 162.

Theoctistus.   Died about 890.
> Jesus ! name all names above.

Theodulph, Saint.   Died 821.   See page 245.
> All glory, laud, and honor.

Thomas of Celano.   Thirteenth century.   See page 248.
> Day of wrath! O day of mourning.

Thring, Godfrey.
> Watch now, ye Christians, watch and pray.

Toke, Emma.   1851.
> O Lord, thou knowest all the snares.

Tomkins, Henry George.
> Come, Lord Jesus, quickly come.

Weiss, Michael.   Died 1540.
> Christ the Lord is risen again.

Weissel, George.   1590–1635.
> The mighty gates of earth unbar.
> Macht hoch das Thor, die Thüren weit

Wesley, Charles.   1708–1788.   See pages 107, 174, 176, and 225.

Wesley, John.   1703–1791.   See page 104.

Wesley, Samuel.   1662–1735.
> Behold the Saviour of mankind.

Wesley, Samuel, Jr.   1690–1739.
> The Lord of Sabbath let us praise.

White, Henry Kirke.   1785–1806.   See page 132.

Whitfield, Frederick.   1829.
> I need thee, precious Jesus.

Whiting, William.   1825.
> Eternal Father, strong to save.

Whittier, John Greenleaf.   1808.
> O Holy Father, just and true.

Whytehead, Thomas.   1815–1843.
> Resting from His work to-day.

Williams, Helen Maria.   1762–1827.

Williams, William.   1717–1791.   See page 30.

Willis, Nathaniel Parker.   1807–1862.
> The perfect world by Adam trod.

Wilson, Caroline.   1787–1846.
> Often the clouds of deepest woe.

Winkler, J. J.   1670–1722.
> Shall I, for fear of feeble man ?
> Sollt' ich aus Furcht vor Menschenkindern.

Wither, George.   1588–1667.
> Come, O come, with sacred lays.

Wittenmyer, Annie.
> I have entered the valley of blessings so sweet.

Wood, J. Riddall.
> As streams that from the fountain flow.

Woodd, Basil.   1760–1831.
> Blest be Jehovah, mighty Lord.

Woodford, James Russell.
>> Thee we adore, O hidden Saviour.
>> Adoro Te devoté, latens Deitas.

Wordsworth, C.   1807.
>> O day of rest and gladness.

Wrangham, William.   Died 1832.
>> To thee, my righteous King and Lord.

Wreford, J. Reynell.
>> Lord, while for all mankind we pray.

Wright, Philip James.   1810–1863.
>> The Lord of glory left his throne.

Wyatt, Henry Herbert.
>> God, the Lord, has heard our prayer.

Xavier, Francis.   1506–1552.   See page 71.
>> My God, I love thee; not because.
>> O Deus, ego amo te.

Young, Andrew.   1810.   See page 146.

Zinzendorf, N. L.   1700–1760.   See page 99.